The Men Who Made

HIBERNIAN FC
SINCE 1946

The Men Who Made

HIBERNIAN FC
SINCE 1946

Jim Jeffrey

TEMPUS

First published 2005

Tempus Publishing Ltd
The Mill, Brimscombe Port
Stroud, Gloucestershire GL5 2QG

© Jim Jeffrey, 2005

British Library Cataloguing in Publication Data.
A catalogue record for this book is available from the British Library.

ISBN 0 7524 3091 2

Typesetting and origination by Tempus Publishing
Printed and bound in Great Britain

CONTENTS

ACKNOWLEDGEMENTS

The aim of this book was always to paint as full a picture of the players as possible. Thus I went well beyond their Hibernian experiences in detailing their careers. I could not have done this without the help of club historians from other outfits. In this respect I must thank the likes of Duncan Carmichael at Ayr United, Alastair MacLachlan at St Mirren, Pat Woods at Celtic, Robert McElroy at Rangers, Peter Rundo at Dundee United, Genge Fry at Motherwell, John Glencross at Alloa and Rob Mason at Sunderland.

However, this book is first and foremost a reminiscence about time spent absorbed with Hibernian and therefore it is to Stewart Crowther, John Campbell, Brian Johnson, John Gibson, David Hardie (*Edinburgh Evening News*) and Simon Pia (*The Scotsman*) that I owe my greatest debt. They have watched Hibs in various capacities and their astute observations and willingness to recollect the players was an enormous help to me.

I would also like to thank all of the players whom I interviewed over the years when compiling the Hibernian match programme. In particular I owe much to Pat Stanton, Lawrie Reilly and Jackie McNamara; all three have been unfailingly helpful whenever I have asked for their time over the years and they are a credit to the game and to Hibernian.

PHOTOGRAPHIC ACKNOWLEDGEMENTS

The images used in this book have come from scrapbooks, albums and photographs owned by former players and club officials and my own collection. I am particularly grateful to Lawrie Reilly who allowed me to borrow his stunning career scrapbooks. I am also much indebted to Elaine Morrison of Hibernian Football Club for arranging with SNSPix of Glasgow for additional images.

The West Stand before redevelopment.

INTRODUCTION

Hibernian Football Club is an integral part of Edinburgh's sporting fabric. Over the years many of Scotland's finest players have pulled on the famous green and white jersey of Hibernian – Gordon Smith, Lawrie Reilly, John Collins and Andy Goram to name but a few. But this book is a celebration of all the players who have turned out for Hibernian since 1946.

I have attempted in words to capture the essence of those players, be they international stars like Joe Baker or mere 'one game wonders'. Each and every one of them has contributed in part to the story of Hibs. The goals, the games, the saves, the drama, all rely on one thing… the players.

This is not intended to be a dry statistical account therefore I have restricted such details to the bare minimum, but I did feel that knowing how many League games and goals could be attributed to each player was useful. Those figures are up to date as at the end of the 2003/04 season. In the appendix I have included several tables and charts to supplement the brief entry under each player.

Several players in this book have indeed made only a handful of appearances for Hibs, but they merit their place. Professional football is a hard game and injuries, stiff competition and conflicting interests take their toll. Ian Hendry broke his leg just 20 seconds into his debut, and that in a nutshell encapsulates the cruel side of the game. Arthur Duncan, on the other hand, played over 400 games for Hibernian, earned a testimonial match and became a Hibs legend.

Thus all the Hibees who have made a League appearance since the end of the Second World War are included, because they have all played a part in the on-going story at Easter Road.

If anyone has any further information to add to the profiles it would be gratefully received. I had to conclude the book at some point and chose the end of the 2003/04 season but a future update would benefit enormously from the input of Hibernian fans who can add to the story.

A

ADAIR Gerry

Four League outings in season 1973/74 were the extent of Gerry's Hibernian career. He made his bow in a 3–1 win at Dundee in April of that season and looked a solid prospect at centre half. However, the competition offered by Jim Black, Roy Barry and young Derek Spalding was too stiff for an inexperienced youngster. A former West Bromwich Albion apprentice, he left Hibs in the summer of 1975 and subsequently played for Dunfermline, Meadowbank and Armadale.

Appearances: 4 Goals: 0

AGATHE Didier

A former Raith Rovers and Montpellier striker, Didier arrived at Easter Road on a three-month contract at the start of the 2000/01 season and was an instant sensation. Pacy, direct, and a great goalscorer he was quite simply 'electric'. After missing 'a sitter' in his debut at Hearts he then bagged braces against both Dundee clubs. Hibs at this stage were 'flying' and rarely had a season opened with such optimism.

Sadly, Hibs had not signed Didier on a longer contract and as his meteoric rise continued he was snatched away by Celtic. His loss was a tragedy not only for a free scoring Hibs but arguably also for Scottish football as Celtic used him as a wing-back rather than as an exciting striker as Alex McLeish had at Easter Road.

Appearances: 5 Goals: 4

AIRD Peter

In the immediate post-war era Peter Aird was a regular in the Hibernian side. He missed just a single match in the first full season after the Second World War but thereafter gradually slipped out of the side. His career as a post-war Hibee ran from 1946 to 1950 and saw him make 44 appearances. Peter, who came from Cardenden, had been signed in 1943 from Bowhill Rovers. He moved to East Fife in January 1950 and later played in Wales with Caerphilly Town.

Appearances: 44 Goals: 0

AITKEN Andy

Born in Edinburgh in August 1934, Andy was raised in Craigmillar but caught the eye of Hibs while doing his National Service in Northern Ireland and playing for Cliftonville. He joined Hibs in 1955 and, despite being a bit of a late starter at twenty-one years of age, adapted well to his new surroundings.

A clever winger, he was both brave and incisive and a tremendous worker. He made his debut at such short notice against Falkirk that he had to play in a pair of boots borrowed from the great Gordon Smith. In later years he said to me: 'I was so proud to have worn Gordon's boots that I wanted to take them home and put them in a glass case!'

He was a key player by the time the 1958 Scottish Cup final against Clyde came around and his injury in that game badly affected Hibs' hopes. He scored in Lawrie Reilly's final game for the club and then in September 1959 joined West Bromwich Albion.

He scored twice in 22 games for Albion where his time was badly compromised by injury. A return to Scotland saw him help Falkirk gain promotion and Raith Rovers reach a Scottish Cup semi-final. His final club was Gala Fairydean.

Appearances: 35 Goals: 11

AITKENHEAD Johnny

Nicknamed 'The Daddler' Johnny was a tricky outside left. Signed from Queen's Park in 1945 he could well have been a Hibernian legend had his spell at Easter Road not coincided with the forward line known collectively as 'The

Didier Agathe.

Famous Five'. Aitkenhead did make his mark with Hibs but it would be his 1949 transfer to Motherwell, after recovering from a serious leg injury, that made his career.

There was definitely a sense of irony when Johnny played in the 'Well side which beat Hibernian in the 1950 League Cup final at Hampden Park. He missed out on a remarkable cup double that season as Motherwell lost 0–1 to Celtic in the Scottish Cup final. However, he made up for the disappointment by playing in the 1952 team that won Motherwell's first ever Scottish Cup.

Capped three times by the Scottish League, Johnny was a penalty expert and enjoyed a spell in which he netted 40 consecutive penalties. He brought the curtain down on his senior career with a brief spell at Hamilton Academicals.

Appearances: 22 Goals: 10

ALLAN Thomson

Started his career with Hibernian but made his most notable impact on the game while with Dundee, where he won two Scotland caps and a League Cup winner's badge. He did return to Hibs later in his career but only in an emergency as cover.

Thomson made his Hibs debut in demanding circumstances – against Hearts in a Scottish Cup tie in 1966.

By the time his career came to a close he had played with Dundee, St Johnstone, Hearts and, briefly, with Meadowbank Thistle on loan.

Appearances: 70 Goals: 0

ALLEN Willie

In season 1950/51 Willie made one League appearance. That was to be his total Hibernian career. He worked as a miner in Kelty and lived near Lochgelly.

In May 1952 this right-winger joined Stirling Albion where he stayed for six months, making six appearances, before stepping down from senior football.

Appearances: 1 Goals: 0

ALLISON Ken

Signed from West Calder United in 1958, Ken was listed as an inside left. In season 1958/59 he played five League games and scored four goals. He also scored in the 3–0 home friendly win over Bayern Munich. It is therefore rather surprising that he had such a short Easter Road career.

After Hibs his football took him to Cowdenbeath, Darlington and Lincoln City. He was particularly successful at Darlington where his incisive inside forward play earned him 39 goals from just 75 starts. Ken was born in Edinburgh in January 1937.

Appearances: 5 Goals: 4

ANDERSON Des

A schoolboy internationalist, Des was lured to Hibs in 1957 from Edinburgh Thistle. Sadly, two League outings in 1957/58 was the sum total of Des Anderson's career with Hibs. Although signed as a centre forward he achieved more as a wing half but he was eventually frustrated by the lack of opportunity at Hibernian and in June 1961 moved south to join Millwall. He spent two seasons in London and made 46 League outings for the Lions.

Appearances: 2 Goals: 0

ANDERSON Derek

Signed by Alex McLeish during Hibernian's brief stint in the First Division, Derek was a journeyman centre half who figured in six games while on loan. The last of his matches was a 3–3 draw with Ayr United and did not go quite the way Derek had anticipated.

He had played with Kilmarnock and Ayr United prior to his Easter Road adventure. He went to Morton after his loan spell in

Edinburgh ended and thereafter had stints with Alloa and Queen of the South.
Appearances: 6 Goals: 0

ANDERSON Bill

Season 1953/54 saw Bill enter the category marked 'one game wonders'. His father had served Hibs and Bill joined the club after having starred for Bishop Auckland at Wembley in the English Amateur Cup final and won six Amateur Scotland caps. He was an inside right and stood six feet tall. Bill later played with Southend United and Weymouth.
Appearances: 1 Goals: 0

ANDERSSON Daniel

A Swedish goalkeeper, Daniel turned out for Ramlosa, Angelholm, Kalmar, Hogaborg and Trelleborgs before joining Hibs from AIK Stockholm in February 2003.

He made his Hibernian debut against Celtic at Parkhead on 2 March 2003 and impressed despite conceding a last minute goal in a 2–3 defeat. An excellent shot-stopper he pulled off one of the great saves of recent years against Partick Thistle when denying Derek Fleming at a free-kick. He was capped once by Sweden but he left Hibs in 2004.
Appearances: 41 Goals: 0

ANDREWS Lyndon

An internationalist with Trinidad & Tobago, Lyndon joined Hibernian from the bizarrely named Joe Public in the summer of 2000; his previous club was the equally exotically titled Superstar Rangers. A tricky midfield schemer, Lyndon's career at Easter Road never quite took off and despite some invigorating displays he was never a permanent feature in the Hibs first team. He made his debut against Stenhousemuir in a League Cup tie in August 2000. Released in April 2002 Lyndon took up an offer to train in Belgium.
Appearances: 12 Goals: 0

ARCHIBALD Steve

A teenage sensation with Clyde (whom he joined from East Stirlingshire), Steve spent three years at Shawfield before joining Aberdeen in 1978. He was a huge success at Pittodrie and it cost Tottenham £800,000 to lure him to London. Equally successful at Spurs his next port of call was the mighty Spanish giants Barcelona where he fully justified a then huge transfer fee (£1.5 million). He spent a short spell on loan to the less salubrious Blackburn before Hibernian signed him.

He made his Hibs debut in a Skol Cup tie against Stranraer in August 1988 and scored twice in a 4–0 win. Steve played in 44 Premier League matches for Hibs and his experience and skill were a huge benefit to those around him. After his stint at Hibs this often underrated Scotland international enjoyed playing with an array of clubs – Espanyol, St Mirren, Reading, Fulham, Ayr United, Clyde, and Dublin-based Home Farm.

He later became a successful football agent, managed East Fife and was also involved in the first bid to save Airdrie in 1999. His curriculum vitae includes an entry as a director at Portuguese giants Benfica.
Appearances: 44 Goals: 15

ARPINON Freddy

Signed in March 2001 by Alex McLeish from French side Troyes, Freddy had trained with Hibernian at the start of that season but was unable to achieve release from his club. A vastly experienced midfielder he had a mixture of creativity and aggression about his play.

His French career also included time with Nimes, Metz and Strasbourg. When he finally arrived at Hibernian the club were heading for third place in the League and for a place in the Scottish Cup final and he found it hard to break into a settled side.

A nippy midfielder, he was quite willing to 'put himself about' and was booked just minutes into his debut. He later earned a degree of notoriety for being sent off at Dundee after spitting at an opponent. Overall it would also be fair to say that Freddy's time at Easter Road was badly compromised by a string of injuries.

Appearances: 35 Goals: 2

AULD Bertie

Bertie was one of the select band of players who later managed the club. He had made his name with Celtic as a member of the 1967 Lisbon Lions side and arrived at Easter Road in the early 1970s when he was clearly a 'veteran' footballer. However, he was still possessed of a shrewd footballing brain and helped the club win at Ibrox soon after arriving.

His forte, however, was to be coaching and he earned his spurs at Easter Road before going on to be a very successful manager of Partick Thistle. His achievement at Firhill was to keep an unfashionable club in the cut-throat ten-club Premier League.

With hindsight it was perhaps unfortunate that this survival success was based largely on a rigid defensive policy. When Bertie came

Bertie Auld.

back to Hibs in 1980 as boss and adopted these 'safety first' tactics he was not always popular. The lynchpin of his success at Partick had been Alan Rough's goalkeeping and Hibernian had good cause to celebrate Rough's eventual arrival at Easter Road.

Auld was born in Glasgow in March 1938 and his playing career also included a spell with Birmingham City.

Appearances: 9 Goals: 3

B

BAILEY Lee

A youngster at Hibernian in the early 1990s, Lee was unable to establish himself despite making a promising debut at Easter Road against Aberdeen as a nineteen-year-old. Standing at just 5ft 6in tall he was released by Alex Miller having been apparently deemed too small to make the grade.

From Hibs he moved on to Meadowbank Thistle and then Queen of the South. He later joined Brechin City and combined a useful career there with a day job as a driving instructor before moving to Stirling Albion in March 2001.

By August 2002 he had dropped into the junior ranks, serving Bonnyrigg Rose in the new Super Junior Premier League.

Appearances: 1 Goals: 0

BAILLIE Jonathan

Jonathan made a sensational Hibernian debut when he was catapulted into the first team for the 2003 CIS Cup quarter-final tie against Celtic. He coped admirably with the considerable threat of Henrik Larsson and Chris Sutton as Hibs recorded a memorable 2–1 win. Tall and strong, he was keen to build on that tremendous start to his career but was sent off in his very next outing. Nevertheless he had time on his side to make the correct impression.

Appearances: 2 Goals: 0

BAINES Roy

Born in Derby, Roy served both Celtic and Morton twice in his interesting career. He replaced one of the first American imports to Scotland – Dave Brcic – when he returned to Morton from Hibs.

His spell with Hibs in the early 1970s coincided with that of Gordon Marshall. This meant that the club had two English goalkeepers on their books. Roy, for all his ability, never quite dominated the scene at Easter Road and made only 23 appearances, all of them in the 1970/71 campaign. His stint with Hibs ended in 1972.

Nevertheless, this setback did not deter him and he was still playing football in 1983, joining St Johnstone that year. He was later a publican in the Lothian region.

Appearances: 23 Goals: 0

BAIRD Sammy

Signed in 1960 from Rangers, Sammy was a powerful wing-half. He started his career in Denny before joining Rutherglen Glencairn and then moving to the nearest senior club – Clyde. He won promotion with Clyde in 1952 and moved on to Preston North End before Scott Symon took him to Rangers.

He won League and Scottish Cup honours while at Rangers and had won seven caps at the time Hibernian signed him in 1960. His role was largely to fill the void left by the departure of Bobby Johnstone and encourage the youngsters at Easter Road. He reserved some of his best displays for European nights and would perhaps have stayed longer at Hibernian had an old friend not come calling.

Sammy moved to Third Lanark, managed by ex-Ranger George Young, in November 1962. Alas, Thirds were already showing signs of the malaise that would see them slip from the 'football map' and he moved to Stirling Albion after a brief stay on Glasgow's south side.

Appearances: 38 Goals: 5

BAKER Gerry

Born in New York in 1938, Gerry was with Chelsea at the age of just fifteen before joining Motherwell – where he was extremely unlucky not to be a member of the famous 'Ancell Babes' side.

Unable to oust the likes of Ian St John and Pat Quinn from the Fir Park side he moved to St Mirren in November 1958 for £2,000 and promptly proved himself a most accomplished striker. His Saints debut was a particularly memorable occasion as it was against Hibernian and his elder brother Joe was in the Hibs side. St Mirren won 2–1 that day and Gerry scored the winner.

Gerry Baker.

In 1959 he won a Scottish Cup winner's badge; he scored in every round including the final where the Paisley club beat Aberdeen 3–1. He followed that up with ten goals in a 15–0 Scottish Cup win over Glasgow University the very next season.

In November 1960 he moved to Manchester City for £17,000 but he failed to settle and in November 1961 Hibs paid £18,000 for his services.

Following his elder brother Joe into the team could not have been easy but Gerry was an able marksman and soon rattled in the goals. He topped the Hibernian scoring charts in the 1962/63 season, playing a key role as the club battled against relegation. After a thirteen-match run without a League win Hibs were grateful for his hat-trick against Dundee and a few weeks later he scored the crucial goal in a 1–0 victory over Motherwell. Without his input it is doubtful if Hibs would have avoided relegation.

Gerry was an exciting player and one who always provoked interest. Tricky, incisive and possessing the goal-grabber's single-tracked desire, he was a valuable player but one who was perhaps just a little too self-centred.

He seldom stayed anywhere for long and so it proved at Hibernian. Anxious to exploit his worth he asked for a move and in early December 1963 he was sold to Ipswich Town for £17,000. This was the start of a spell that saw him serve Coventry City and non-League Margate and Nuneaton before going to work for Jaguar in Coventry.

There was a sporting enthusiasm running through his family and his daughters, Karen and Lorraine, were both notable athletes, Lorraine finishing fifth in the Los Angeles 800 metres Olympics race.

Appearances: 59 Goals: 27

BAKER Joe

Joseph Henry Baker – one of the greatest footballers ever to pull on a Hibernian shirt.

Joe Baker.

The first man from outside of the English League to be capped by England was simply sensational. He scored a remarkable 113 League goals for Hibs in only 139 starts.

Born in Liverpool in 1940 his family moved to Wishaw when he was a youngster and he joined Hibernian when just fifteen years old. Hibs quickly 'farmed' him out to junior side Armadale in order to gain experience. From time to time he would feature in the Hibernian reserve side and in the very week that Hibs made their European Cup bow, young Joe was scoring four for the reserves in a 10–1 win – he was still six months short of his sixteenth birthday.

When he broke into the first team as a seventeen-year-old he was remarkably quickly among the goals. Joe made his debut against

Airdrie at Broomfield in a League Cup tie and went on to score a scarcely credible 31 goals in his first senior season.

Selecting his greatest feat is no mean task. He would earn national fame when scoring all four Hibs goals in a 4–3 Scottish Cup triumph over Hearts at Tynecastle. There was possibly greater fame still to come when he scored nine goals in a single Scottish Cup tie and perhaps yet more in bagging 41 League goals (from just 33 games) in season 1959/60.

He was capped by England at Under-23 and then full international level while a Hibee and he scored on his full debut against Northern Ireland in 1959. Given that he was a contemporary of the likes of Brian Clough, Jimmy Greaves and Bobby Charlton his achievements should never be understated. In short, Joe was a real 'Roy of the Rovers' figure, a sensation in the truest sense of the word and a player for whom the superlatives were quickly exhausted.

The inevitable came, when having been top Hibs goalscorer for four consecutive seasons, he was sold to the Italian giants Torino in July 1961 for £73,000. Although paired with Denis Law in Turin he did not settle and in 1962 returned to Britain with Arsenal for the then incredible sum of £67,000. He later played for Nottingham Forest and Sunderland (1969–71).

In January 1971 he returned to Hibernian, nine years and eight months after his initial departure, and made an impressive second debut, scoring with a classical header in a 2–1 win over Aberdeen – a match that ended the Dons remarkable run of fifteen straight wins.

Injuries however had caught up with Joe and he retired soon afterwards, although there was time for a brief sortie to Raith Rovers and an incredible 25 League goals from only 24 matches in season 1972/73.

After his playing career was over Joe dabbled in football management, firstly in the junior ranks with Fauldhouse United then in the senior game with Albion Rovers in two short spells in 1981 and 1984.

Finally, more detailed mention must be made of the nine-goal haul Joe had in 1961 against Peebles Rovers in the Scottish Cup. Twelve months earlier his brother Gerry had bagged ten for St Mirren against Glasgow University. Thus a pair of brothers bagged nineteen Scottish Cup goals between them in two Scottish Cup ties. The chances of that being repeated are slim to say the least!

Sadly Joe died in October 2003. His death was greatly mourned at Easter Road and indeed at all of his former clubs.

Appearances: 139 Goals: 113

BANNERMAN Scott

Signed by Alex Miller in 1995 from Hutcheson Vale BC, Scott played a handful of games for Alex McLeish and ultimately left for Morton.

Scott was a midfielder and was a close relative of former Hearts favourite John Robertson.

Appearances: 13 Goals: 0

BANNON Eamonn

Born in Edinburgh in 1958, Eamonn enjoyed a marvellous playing career that took in Hearts, Chelsea, Dundee United and then both Hearts and Hibs before his playing 'twilight' stint with Stenhousemuir.

While at Tannadice he really flourished and he was an integral part of their Championship and League Cup winning sides. Moreover, he served Scotland 11 times and played in some wonderful European nights.

He was briefly a player coach at Hibs and then assistant manager at Hearts before donning his boots again for Terry Christie's Stenhousemuir. A fairytale ending saw him bow out with a Challenge Cup winner's medal, ironically gained against Dundee United.

His football career ended in a note of controversy as he was sacked as manager of Falkirk after the Bairns had used an unregistered player in a match against St Mirren, thus incurring a steep Scottish League fine. There are many who felt that the responsibility for fielding the player did not lie at Eamonn's door.

Appearances: 1 Goals: 0

BARRY Roy

A powerful centre half, Roy ended his senior career at Hibernian, having started it across the city with Hearts.

His career began with a move from Musselburgh Athletic to Tynecastle. He then joined Dunfermline and was part of the Pars side that defeated Hearts in the 1968 Scottish Cup final (Alex Edwards was also in that side). If that was the high point of his Scottish career, he enjoyed a successful spell in England when he moved to Coventry City and then on to Crystal Palace. It was from Palace that Hibernian boss Eddie Turnbull signed him during the 1974/75 season, just as Roy seemed destined to take up a coaching spot in America. Roy made 36 League outings for Hibs between 1974 and 1976.

Appearances: 36 Goals: 0

BAXTER John

At 5ft 11in and 12st in weight, John was a powerful half-back who joined Hibernian from Benburb in 1955. He could defend with vigour but liked to get forward too and netted some memorable goals, including one against Rangers in the late 1950s.

John played 209 League matches for Hibs between 1957 and 1966. He was capped by Scotland at Under-23 level against Wales in 1958 and was considered by many to be unlucky not to build on that international experience.

Although signed in 1955 he had to wait two years – courtesy of National Service – to make

John Baxter.

his Hibs debut. He proved a popular figure in the dressing room at Easter Road and, as Lawrie Reilly recalled: 'He was a dependable laddie, with great strength. He had a strong chin and real physical presence, in some ways he had an almost "Desperate Dan" look about him. John was always good for morale and while not spectacular or flashy as a player he was very consistent.'

It was his reliability and longevity that convinced Falkirk to sign him at the tail end of his career. He teamed up with Doug Baillie there in what must have been one of the most fearsome defences in the Scottish game. From Falkirk it was on to Clydebank before retiring.

Appearances: 209 Goals: 23

BEAUMONT Dave

Began his career with Dundee United in 1980 and rapidly progressed through the ranks. He helped Scotland win the Under-18 European Championship in 1983 and represented Dundee United in the 1987 UEFA Cup final.

Dave joined Luton Town after eight years on Tayside and helped his new club reach the 1989 League Cup final. He joined Hibs in October 1991 and was on the bench as Hibernian won the League Cup final weeks later. However, injury disrupted his Easter Road career and it is fair to say the Hibs support never saw the best of him in his four years at the club.

Appearances: 70 Goals: 2

BEEDIE Stuart

A very solid midfielder, Stuart gave service to several clubs in a lengthy career. He started with Montrose then moved to St Johnstone for £20,000 in 1981.

However, Stuart was signed for Hibs from Dundee United. He played a major part in the infamous clash with Rangers at the start of the 1986/87 season. Rangers' new player/manager Graeme Souness was sent off at Easter Road for his 'assault' on George McCluskey, an incident that had its roots in a challenge by Beedie on Souness. Beedie scored in that game and Hibs went on to claim a famous 2–1 victory.

His time with Hibs was followed by spells at Dunfermline and Dundee in a career, which, at times, resembled an East Coast Safari.

Appearances: 9 Goals: 2

BELL Dougie

Signed for £30,000 in 1987 the former St Mirren, Aberdeen and Rangers midfielder was a cultured player who had made his name as part and parcel of Alex Ferguson's Aberdeen reign. He was probably past his best when he joined Hibs and later he served Shrewsbury Town and Hull City.

Appearances: 32 Goals: 2

BEST George

Let us be clear from the outset. In the list of Hibernian players who have given their all for the club, George Best would hardly figure. His presence at Easter Road was, in short, a cameo appearance. However, he was an international superstar, well known even outwith football. Thus to ignore his, albeit short, presence at Easter Road is not possible.

Born in Belfast in 1946, George Best was one of the greatest post-war European footballers. A left-winger of extraordinary skill he was also one of the most famous personalities of the 'Beatles' era. Sadly it was an inability to handle this exposure to the limelight that ultimately ended his football career prematurely.

Capped 37 times by Northern Ireland, Best was one of Matt Busby's great Manchester United team that could boast talents such as Bobby Charlton and Denis Law. He won a European Cup medal in 1968; indeed, he scored in the final against Benfica. In that year he was both English and European Footballer of the Year. In short he was world class.

However, he was not a dedicated professional and was finally released from Old Trafford and played with the likes of Fulham and Fort Lauderdale before Hibernian signed him in November 1979.

His Hibs debut came against St Mirren at Paisley and the gate was hugely swelled (over 13,000 turned up compared to 8,000 for the same fixture in the previous season!). Hibs lost 2–1 but Best scored the Hibees' counter and a love affair was born. Over 20,000 turned up at Easter Road for an otherwise mundane match against Partick Thistle as he made his Edinburgh debut.

Yet for all the glitz George brought to Easter Road, the sad fact was that the club was firmly entrenched in the basement spot of the Premier Division. Best was hardly likely to prove a miracle worker, particularly as he was posted absent so often. His appearances were sporadic and Edinburgh was 'ablaze' with rumours about Best's off field antics. In January 1980 he briefly banished such talk by scoring

George Best.

a wonderful effort in a 1–1 draw with Celtic but soon he was up to his old tricks again.

Hibs were patient with the wayward Irish genius but he failed to apply himself and was soon on his way. He was transferred to San Jose in February 1980 but had a final farewell in October 1980 having returned from his loan spell and action in the American League.

That final outing came against Falkirk and was the result of a shrewd deal on the part of Hibs. When American soccer agent Dennis Roach secured George Best's contract from Hibernian it not only cost him £30,000 but had the proviso that Best had to make one last appearance as a Hibee. Hibs further milked the occasion by making Best captain for the day.

Chairman Tom Hart had shown remarkable vision in bringing Best to Easter Road and Hibs had gained enormous publicity.

Appearances: 17 Goals: 3

BEUZELIN Guillaume

A twenty-five-year old French midfielder, Guillame was signed by Tony Mowbray at the start of the 2004/05 season. Having previously played with Le Havre and Beauvais in France, he was a seasoned campaigner and made an immediate impression with his incisive passing and calm approach in the helter-skelter of the SPL midfield battle-zone.

BLACK Ian

A left-back, Ian was a youngster in the Hibernian team at the start of the First Division campaign in 1980/81. He played in the first half of the season making two appearances.
Appearances: 2 Goals: 0

BLACK Jim

Jim scored an own goal against Hibs while an Airdrie player in 1968, but it is doubtful if that lay behind his £30,000 transfer to Hibs in 1969. Rather his immaculate showing in a Third Round Scottish Cup tie when Airdrie beat Hibs 1–0 probably did the trick.

A tall centre half he had joined Airdrie from Lochend Hearts in 1962. He made his Easter Road debut against Newcastle United in August 1969. He proved a good buy for Hibernian and won a League Cup winner's badge in 1972. He was also a key performer in the two Dryburgh Cup wins over Celtic around the same time.

He linked very well with John Blackley at the back and, although not among the better known of the Turnbull side, he was undoubtedly a vital cog.

Remarkably injury free, he enjoyed a run of well over 100 consecutive matches and was an extremely contented footballer. Offered the chance to go to England he turned it down saying he liked living in Airdrie. This was clearly true because he returned to

Jim Black.

Airdrie when his Hibs career ended after five years.
Appearances: 151 Goals: 0

BLACKLEY John

A wonderfully composed defender, 'Sloop' joined Hibs in 1964 from Gairdoch United and went on to have a great Hibs career. He was part of the super Turnbull's Tornadoes side and marshalled his defensive colleagues with assurance and no little style.

He played in some memorable Hibernian matches, including the 7–0 rout of Hearts at Tynecastle and the 6–1 European hammering of Sporting Lisbon. By the early 1970s he was easily one of Scotland's finest central defenders and he graduated from league internationals to full internationals very quickly. Indeed, he played for Scotland in the 1974 World Cup finals in Germany.

Sold to Newcastle United for £100,000 in October 1977 he was highly appreciated at St James' Park until moving on to Preston and Hamilton (as player/manager eventually)

John Blackley in action against Motherwell at Fir Park.

before returning to Hibs and ultimately managing the club.

Appointed Hibs boss in September 1984, Blackley stayed until his resignation in the winter of 1986, arguably having expected to achieve too much too soon.

John's love of football remained undiminished and he worked as a coach at Dundee United and St Johnstone after leaving Easter Road. The nickname 'Sloop' was a reference to the popular Beach Boys hit 'Sloop John B'.

Appearances: 279 Goals: 6

BLAIR Jim

A centre forward, Jim was signed from St Mirren in June 1970. He had bagged 18 goals for the Saints in the 1969/70 season and was a powerful six footer. What's more he had only been part-time at Paisley, working as a chemical operator during the day.

Sadly he never lived up to his undoubted promise and went back to Saints in February 1971 having failed to settle. He played in 15 League games for Hibs and did score a few in the autumn of 1970, including two in a 3–2 win over Rangers at Easter Road. He had initially joined St Mirren in 1967 from Shotts Bon Accord and was a one-time Scottish junior badminton champion!

Appearances: 15 Goals: 5

BOCO Jimmy

One thing must be clarified from the outset. Known as 'Jimmy Boco' to the Hibernian support, his real name was Jean Marc Adjoui Boco.

Signed from Lens at the start of the 1997/98 season he made 29 outings in that strange campaign, which started with a scintillating home win over Celtic but ended in relegation. He did not survive and played no part in the Alex McLeish revival of Hibs.

Appearances: 29 Goals: 0

BOGIE Malcolm

In 1955 Malcolm represented Scotland Schoolboys against England at Liverpool and this ensured a host of clubs chased his signature. Hibs convinced him to come to Easter Road and the apprentice engineer finally made the move in 1956, signing from Balgreen Rovers. Two games in the 1958/59 season and one in the 1962/63 season was the disappointing sum of his Hibs League career.

He joined Grimsby Town in July 1963 but played just one match for the Mariners (and two on loan with Aldershot) before winding down his career.

Appearances: 3 Goals: 0

BOTTIGLIERI Emilio

This young Canadian player was signed in September 1997 from Metro Ford and never quite made the hoped-for impact. He enjoyed a rousing debut against Barnsley when the supporters, intrigued by his unusual surname, cheered his every move. However, such popularity could not sustain him in the first team and he eventually left to join Morton. He played a single game in Hibs' 1998/99 promotion run.

Appearances: 1 Goals: 0

BOYLE George

Signed as a right-back from Ballieston Juniors in 1949, George showed great patience while at Hibs. Between 1953 and 1959 he made a clutch of appearances. He would probably have made more than 11 appearances were competition, provided by the likes of Govan and Howie, not quite so stiff

Appearances: 11 Goals: 0

BRAZIL Ally

A cult hero amongst Hibernian fans, it would be fair to say that Brazil was not the most skilled footballer during his lengthy stay at Easter Road but certainly one of the most reliable and popular. His approach to the game was of the no frills variety and he lacked nothing in effort or enthusiasm.

Eddie Turnbull signed Brazil from Currie Hearts in December 1976 on the recommendation of scout John Smart; but only after two trial games. Indeed, Turnbull never quite seemed 'sold' on 'Benny' until John Lambie the Hibernian assistant coach pushed his case.

Encouraged by Lambie's faith the youngster was blooded and by 1979 he had made sufficient progress to play in the Scottish Cup final against Rangers. His debut had come against Aberdeen at Pittodrie in 1977.

Ally built upon that debut and went on to play, largely in defence, in over 200 matches during a Hibernian career that lasted a decade. He was never a regular goalscorer but cemented his quirky reputation when he scored not once, not twice, but a hat-trick in a friendly against Celtic in the 1984/85 season.

The fact that John Lambie had championed Brazil's cause proved profitable for Ally in the mid-1980s. As his playing career at Easter Road drew to a close Lambie recruited him

Ally Brazil.

for Hamilton Academicals. Accies were newly promoted to the Premier League and Lambie rightly identified the need for an experienced defender as a priority. Ally was a member of the Hamilton side that quite sensationally knocked Rangers out of the Scottish Cup in 1987.

Despite that marvellous experience, Ally never really settled at Douglas Park and he moved to Forfar Athletic. Those who thought his career would rapidly conclude were in for a pleasant surprise as Brazil made over 150 outings for Forfar before moving down into the junior ranks.
Appearances: 202 Goals: 8

BREBNER Grant

Born in 1977 in Edinburgh, Grant's midfield promise was such that he was capped 18 times by Scotland at Under-21 level. His senior career began with Manchester United and he initially joined Hibs on loan at the tail end of the 1999 relegation season.

Despite his finest efforts, and an excellent goal against Dundee United, he was unable to

help Hibs stay in the Premier League and in the summer of 1998 elected to join Tommy Burns' Reading, with Manchester United receiving £300,000 in exchange.

The 1998/99 season saw him in fine form for Reading and he scored 10 League goals but did not settle and decided to return to Hibs, this time on a full-time basis in the summer of 1999. Slipping into a midfield that could boast the likes of Latapy and Sauzee he flourished. Strong running Brebner added work-rate to an engine room that was rich in flair.

His Hibs career did not always run smoothly and at one stage he spent a period on loan with Stockport County. More serious was a triple arm fracture sustained in a cup-tie against Rangers at Easter Road.

Early in the 2003/04 season he joined that small group of players who have had a red card decision rescinded. In Grant's case the red card picked up in the 1–0 win over Hearts was overturned on the strength of television evidence.

He remained an influential player with Hibs until his transfer to Ian McCall's Dundee United in September 2004. What was his finest game as a Hibee? Easy – scoring a hat-trick in a 3–2 Scottish Cup win over Dundee United at Tannadice in 2002.
Appearances: 130 Goals: 7

BREMNER Des

Enthusiastic, committed and skilful – those are the qualities most readily associated with the career of Des Bremner at Hibs.

Born in Aberchirder in 1952, Des joined Hibs from Deveronvale in 1972. He went on to become one of the most versatile and determined midfielders at Easter Road and enjoyed a lengthy spell with the club before moving to Aston Villa. That September 1979 transfer was a Hibernian record, with the Birmingham-based club paying £275,000.

Grant Brebner.

Des Bremner.

With Villa Des scaled the heights by winning the European Cup and the English Championship.

Des made his Hibs debut against Dundee United in January 1973. Capped by Scotland at Youth, Under-23 and full international level he had boundless energy and enthusiasm. He made his Scotland debut against Switzerland in a 1–0 win, coming on for Kenny Dalglish, and added his full cap to Scottish League awards.

In total Des made 200 League appearances for Hibs. His career in England took in not only Aston Villa, but also their great city rivals Birmingham. Unusually he was held in high esteem by both halves of the Birmingham divide.

After retiring from playing Des worked for the English PFA. His brother Kevin was also a notable player.

Appearances 200: Goals: 18

BREWSTER Craig

The ex-Forfar, Raith and Dundee United striker joined Hibs in July 2001 from Greek side Ionikos. Vastly experienced, Craig had scored the winner in the 1994 Scottish Cup final for United. His stint in Greece improved his range of skills and few players held and distributed the ball with such assurance.

He proved a great foil for young Garry O'Connor but in a harsh economic climate Bobby Williamson had to release Craig and he moved to Dunfermline in the summer of 2002. Late in 2004 he joined Inverness as manager.

Appearances: 25 Goals: 3

BROGAN John

A £15,000 capture from St Johnstone, where he had been their all-time top goalscorer, Hibs chased long and hard to land this marksman. Indeed, in 1980, when Brogan walked out on St Johnstone briefly, Hibs offered £120,000 for his services and were astonished when this was rejected. When that deal collapsed Brogan returned to the fold at Saints and promptly scored seven goals in only nine games.

Sadly, for all the effort of the chase, his stay with Hibs was short and slightly disappointing. He later played with Hamilton and Stirling Albion before managing the latter and Arbroath. By the year 2002 he was manager of junior club East Kilbride Thistle.

Appearances: 5 Goals: 1

BROWN John

Signed from Clyde in May 1942 John, who was a goalkeeper, played for Hibs in the immediate post-war period. He had a single appearance in the 1946/47 campaign and added a further 11 in the 1947/48 season.

In January 1948 he was transferred to Dundee having spent a brief period on loan with Third Lanark. He later served Tranmere Rovers and Hartlepool. Born and bred in Portobello he was a Scottish Schoolboy internationalist.

Appearances: 12 Goals: 0

BROWN John Y.

John made his only appearance for Hibernian in the 1953/53 season, standing in for Jock Paterson in the match against Partick Thistle on 13 December. It proved to be an unlucky date as Hibs went down 5–4 in an astonishing game.

A Musselburgh lad he moved to Third Lanark on 18 November 1955.

Appearances: 1 Goals: 0

BROWN Jim

Jim was a distinguished full-back for Hearts in the late 1960s and 1970s before moving to Hibernian in 1979. Solid and reliable, his claim to fame, however, was to lie outwith Edinburgh. Jim was on the receiving end of a quite horrendous and sickening tackle by John Pelosi of St Johnstone (this when Brown was briefly at Dunfermline), which ended in a high-profile court case.

Brown's career at Hibs got off to a fine start. Played as a midfielder he scored two goals in his early outings, one against Manchester City in the Skol Cup at Tynecastle and one against St Mirren in an Anglo-Scottish Cup tie; the latter being on his debut.

He played with Hibs for two seasons, the first of which saw Hibs relegated and the second promoted, so they were hardly dull years. As mentioned above he then moved to Dunfermline.

Appearances: 44 Goals: 0

BROWN Jim A.

Signed initially on a one-month deal in 1980, Jim stayed for longer when it was clear Bertie Auld admired his midfield talents.

It was unfortunate, not to mention confusing, that his spell at Easter Road should coincide with that of another Jim Brown (ex-Hearts). This particular Brown version had played in Belgium with Ghent and in Greece with Ethnikos. However, he was better known for his spells in England with Portsmouth and Aston Villa.

Appearances: 15 Goals: 1

BROWN Scott

A precocious talent, Scott joined Hibs when he was only thirteen. By the age of seventeen he had burst into the first team with such industry and drive it was clear he was a tremendous prospect.

He was quickly among the goals and the tail end of the 2002/03 season was much the better for his appearance. The following season he picked up from where he left off and his total fearlessness allied to his sheer skill won him admirers well beyond Easter Road.

By 2004 he was a Scotland Under-21 internationalist and a regular in the Hibs first team, holding his place with ease when Tony Mowbray arrived as manager. His combative style did not always endear him to opposition players and fans, and it was suggested by some experienced players that he had rather too much to say for himself on the field.

Appearances: 40 Goals: 6

BROWN Simon

This Chelmsford-born goalkeeper was Tony Mowbray's first signing for Hibs. Recruited from Colchester United, he had joined the Essex club after stints with Tottenham, Lincoln, Aylesbury, Fulham and Kingstonian. Aged twenty-seven when he arrived in Scotland he enjoyed an excellent reputation for shot stopping and his early games for Hibs did nothing to disprove this trait.

John Brownlie.

BROWN Steve

Steve was signed as an 'S' form when only fifteen and gained Scotland Schools caps at both Under-15 and Under-18 levels.

By 1978 he was breaking into the Hibs side. Between 1978 and 1981 he made sporadic League appearances without ever quite being an automatic selection.

Appearances: 18 Goals: 0

BROWNLIE John

A gifted full-back, John Brownlie was perhaps the most naturally talented and athletic player of the Turnbull's Tornadoes era. Pacy, tigerish in the tackle, and creative going forward he was a permanent fixture in the Hibs team for nine years.

Under-23 caps, full international caps, 211 League outings and a League Cup winner's medal were suitable rewards for a player who was, above all else, classy.

John was a provisional signing when he was sixteen and finally joined when Bob Shankly called him up. He made his Hibs debut at Dunfermline when only eighteen in 1968 and was able to net a few goals in his career. Perhaps the most famous was the winner against Rangers in a 1972 League Cup semi-final at Hampden.

He played concurrently for the Under-23s and full international sides before joining Newcastle United in August 1978 in a deal that carried Ralph Callachan from Tyneside to Easter Road.

John later played for Middlesbrough, Hartlepool, Berwick Rangers and Blyth Spartans. He was then manager at Cowdenbeath, East Stirling and Arbroath. As a player he had served Jackie Charlton, Eddie Turnbull, Malcolm Allison and Tommy Docherty, so perhaps his graduation to

management should be no surprise.
Appearances: 211 Goals: 14

BRUCE Alexander T.

Registered with Hibs on 3 July 1948 as an amateur, Bruce made a single League appearance in season 1948/49. His name was not on the list of retained players for the following season.
Appearances: 1 Goals: 0

BRUCE Willie

Signed from Westerton Ams in 1947, this young goalkeeper had a match in the 1950/51 season. He was unusual in that he was a farmer who drifted into football almost by accident and continued to mix farming with football during his time at Easter Road.
Appearances: 3 Goals: 0

BUCHANAN Archie

Archie was one of the unsung heroes of the post-war Hibernian side that won three

Archie Buchanan (third from left, back row) in Hibernian's 1950/51 Scottish League Division 'A' championship-winning squad.

Championships. He was a Hibee for over a decade when Hibs were arguably the best side in Scotland and lent an enviable amount of drive and muscle to that team.

Signed in 1943 from Edinburgh Thistle, he rather handily lived round the corner from Easter Road. He was among the goals in the first official season after the Second World War and kept that up until the 1956/57 season when he finally retired from the Easter Road scene. He went on to play for St Mirren and managed Cowdenbeath.

In all Archie played 205 League games for Hibernian, which was no mean feat in an era when games were less frequent than today. Arguably had he not suffered a bad leg break at Aberdeen in September 1954 his career would have been even more impressive.
Appearances: 205 Goals: 16

BUCHANAN Jock

This redheaded defender started with Edinburgh Waverley before arriving at Hibs in 1954. He was a versatile player and could play either out wide on the right or through the centre.

In February 1960 John moved to Raith Rovers. His career partially overlapped that of Archie Buchanan, which did pose problems for the sports reporters of that day. Jock played 13 League games for Hibs but probably earned his place in the club's history by virtue of being the first Hibee to score a home European goal (against Rott-Weiss Essen). He was a late replacement for Gordon Smith and had actually enjoyed a plate of 'mince and potatoes' before he received an urgent call to hurry along to Easter Road.
Appearances: 13 Goals: 4

BURRIDGE John

Born in Workington in 1951, John was known as 'Budgie' by virtue of his almost non-stop talking. One of the great veterans of the game,

John joined Hibs when he was thirty-nine in 1991 and stayed for two seasons.

He had started his senior career in 1969 with Workington and then played with a further twelve senior clubs as he clocked up a staggering 700 senior appearances. His clubs in order were: Workington, Blackpool, Aston Villa, (Southend United on loan), Crystal Palace, QPR, Wolves, Derby County (on loan), Sheffield United, Southampton, Newcastle, Hibs, Newcastle (again), Scarborough, Lincoln City, Aberdeen, Manchester City, Dumbarton, Falkirk, Ayr United, Notts County, Darlington, Grimsby, Northampton, Queen of the South and Scarborough (for a second spell).

He was frequently described in the Hibernian match programme as a model professional. Extremely fit, he did not smoke or drink and devoted an enormous amount of time to staying in good shape. His finest moment as a Hibee was surely playing in the 1991 League Cup final.
Appearances: 65 Goals: 0

BYRNE Gordon

Between 1980 and 1983 Gordon made just two outings as a substitute. His debut came against St Johnstone in December 1980. His preferred position was wing half.
Appearances: 2 Goals: 0

BYRNE John

In 1958 John Byrne moved from Pollok Juniors to Preston North End. He never played for the Lancashire club and returned north to play with Queen of the South. In May 1961 he headed back south to join Tranmere Rovers and 4 goals in 37 appearances was enough to see him signed by Hibernian.

Recruited in June 1962, John was a left-sided player who could play either inside or outside left. He flitted in and out of the team and played in the infamous League Cup semi-final reversal against Morton at Ibrox in 1963.

He headed back to England in November 1963 with Barnsley and later served both Peterborough and Northampton Town.

Appearances: 23 Goals: 5

C

CAIRNS Jimmy

It was from Dunipace Thistle in 1946 that Hibs signed Jimmy. He broke his leg in 1949 and this badly hampered his career. By the time he had regained full fitness Hibs were on their way to the 1950/51 title and Jimmy was on his way to Third Lanark in January 1952.

He later played with St Johnstone and very briefly managed them for four games in season 1953/54. It is fair to say that Jimmy was a 'hard' character, having completed a game against Rangers with a broken leg on one occasion. During the war he had served with the Royal Navy and he escaped from the *Ghurka* when it was sunk in the Mediterranean in 1942.

Appearances: 55 Goals: 1

CAIG Tony

A powerfully built goalkeeper, Tony joined Hibernian from Charlton Athletic in 2001. His credentials were impressive but he failed to oust Nick Colgan from the number one jersey. A handful of openings were all that came Tony's way and he was the unfortunate man in goal when Hibs were humbled 5–1 at Hearts in August 2002. In 2003 he was offered a golden opportunity to resurrect his career when Newcastle United signed him in a goalkeeping crisis.

Appearances: 14 Goals: 0

CALDWELL Gary

This Stirling-born youngster joined Newcastle United as a sixteen-year-old and made his United debut against Ipswich Town in November 2000. He had good company at Newcastle – not only did Kenny Dalglish sign him but his brother Stephen was also with the Magpies!

Donald Park lured him to Leith on loan while Franck Sauzee was in charge of Hibernian, and he stayed for the tail end of the 2001/02 season, making 12 SPL appearances. During that stay he played well enough to represent Scotland against France and Nigeria.

However, there was little chance of Hibernian being able to offer this young central defender suitable terms when Newcastle United offered him an attractive contract extension.

Gary returned to Newcastle but failed to make the breakthrough and to his Hibs loan spell he could add stints spent at Darlington, Coventry City and Derby County.

Thus Bobby Williamson was able to sign him for a second time on loan in January 2004. This arrangement was finally made permanent during the early stewardship of Tony Mowbray. By this time Gary was a regular in the heart of Berti Vogts' Scotland defence.

Appearances: 28 Goals: 1

CALLACHAN Ralph

The slim left-sided midfielder made his mark with Hearts in the mid-1970s, moved to Newcastle United for a huge fee then returned to the Scottish capital with Hibernian in August 1978.

His move to Easter Road in August 1978 saw popular full-back John Brownlie head for Newcastle as part of a swap deal. That could have been a millstone around his neck but Ralph was a cultured player who, although slightly built, was quickly able to prove his worth at Easter Road.

By playing for Hibs in the 1979 Scottish Cup final he achieved the unusual distinction of

Ralph Callachan.

having represented both Edinburgh sides in Scottish Cup finals. In August 1979 he scored one of the great Easter Road goals when slaloming through the entire Dundee defence before rounding their 'keeper to net. Ralph played 219 League games for Hibs and consistently impressed with his incisive, creative style.

Off the field Ralph was a great friend of Jackie McNamara and they ran a public house together.
Appearances: 219 Goals: 26

CAMERON Ian

Made his League debut for St Mirren in 1983 and won a Scottish Cup medal in 1987. He moved to Aberdeen two years later for £300,000 and his subtle midfield promptings were well received at Pittodrie.

He joined Hibernian in the 1996/97 season, when the club required a play-off victory over Airdrie to preserve its Premier League status. It was, however, from Partick Thistle that Hibs had signed him and as part of that deal Gareth

Evans and David Farrell went to Firhill in exchange.

He joined Airdrie in 2001 following the collapse of the Steve Archibald rescue package and the appointment of Ian McCall as Diamonds' manager.
Appearances: 17 Goals: 0

CAMERON Alex

A centre half, Alex was snapped up from St Bernards 'A' in 1961. However, despite a couple of runs in the team (he made a dozen games in 1962/63 and three games the next season) he was never able to establish his first-team credentials fully. He joined Oldham Athletic in 1964.
Appearances: 15 Goals: 0

CAMPBELL Colin

Born in the Hebridean island of Benbecula in December 1956, Colin was a centre forward who joined Hibs in August 1978. He made his

Colin Campbell.

Ian Cameron.

debut ironically enough in the Highlands – against Inverness Thistle – and was a strong and direct leader.

He played one of his best games for the club in the Scottish Cup final against Rangers in 1979, coming very close to landing the cup for Hibs.

While with Hibs he was studying at Edinburgh University. His subsequent career saw him spend a short spell with Dundee United. He returned to Benbecula to open a sports shop and settle once more in the Outer Hebrides.

Appearances: 38 Goals: 5

CAMPBELL John

John was a left half who arrived at Hibs from Musselburgh Union in 1953. He played just two matches in season 1953/54 and thereafter disappeared from the Easter Road picture.

Appearances: 2 Goals: 0

CARROLL Pat

Raised in Tullibody, right-winger Pat joined Hibs as a seventeen-year-old in 1975. He was an 'S' form and gave a wonderful display for Scotland schools against their English counterparts at Wembley. He had been with Sauchie Juniors before Eddie Turnbull lured him to Edinburgh.

Although he made a few first-team outings he was unable to command a regular starting spot and he moved to Raith Rovers in 1980.

Appearances: 17 Goals: 0

CARSON Tom

Tom joined Hibs on loan from Dundee in 1987 and played in just a couple of games. A solid goalkeeper he enjoyed a lengthy career with both Dumbarton and Dundee.

He joined Raith Rovers and helped them to a promotion, thereby repeating an achievement he enjoyed at both Dundee and Dumbarton.

By 2001 Tom was manager of Dumbarton at their new 'Rock' stadium.

Appearances: 2 Goals: 0

CAUGHEY Mark

Mark was part of the initial Northern Ireland squad for the Mexico '86 World Cup finals. Indeed, he was with the squad in America when Hibs chairman Kenny Waugh flew over to secure his signature.

A winger by trade, he failed to 'set the heather on fire' with Hibs and played in 14 games in 1986/87.

He left Hibs to return to Northern Ireland and was last heard of working as an officer in the RUC.

Appearances: 14 Goals: 0

CHARNLEY Jim 'Chic'

Jim, one of the great characters of the Scottish game, was as well loved by fans as he was 'feared' by referees.

A one-time 'bad boy' of the game his early career took in periods at St Mirren, Ayr United, Pollok Juniors, Clydebank, Partick Thistle, St Mirren (again), Bolton, Partick Thistle, Dumbarton and Dundee before Hibernian came calling.

It was Jim Duffy who signed him in January 1997 and the deal was unusual in that it was a 'pay per game' arrangement. Charnley's was a natural brand of talent and was welded to a sharp temper and a willingness to speak his mind, which often brought him into conflict with authority. Nevertheless, he brightened up the scene at Easter Road.

Chic scored one of the all-time great Hibs goals at the start of the 1997/98 season. In the opening League game against Celtic he struck with an audacious lob as Hibs won 2–1 – quite a memory.

He could not sustain such heroics, however, and his work-rate was never really ideal in the modern game. From Hibs he journeyed to

Chic Charnley up against former Hibee favourite Mickey Weir.

Partick Thistle (for a third spell), Tarff Rovers, Portadown, Kirkintilloch Rob Roy and Partick Thistle once more (for a fourth spell in 2002).

Chic was a noted Celtic fan and had even 'guested' for them in a testimonial match at Manchester United.

Appearances: 29 Goals: 4

CHISHOLM Gordon

Born in Bishopbriggs, Glasgow in 1960 Chisholm went straight from school to Sunderland and played over 200 games for the Rokerites.

Signed from Sunderland for £60,000 in September 1985 he made a sensational Hibs debut, scoring the opening goal in a 2–0 League Cup semi-final win over Rangers. This helped him to achieve the unusual distinction of playing in English and Scottish League Cup finals in the same calendar year.

He was a tall, commanding central defender and gave Hibs experience in a key position. It was little wonder John Blackley was keen to sign him as Gordon could also play the holding midfield role.

From Hibs (for whom he made 59 League outings between 1985 and 1988) he moved to Dundee and Partick Thistle before eventually finding a career in coaching working with Ian McCall at Dundee United.

Appearances: 59 Goals: 4

CLARK Willie

Signed in 1939 from Bonnyrigg Rose, Willie was making good progress when he suffered a bad leg injury in a pre-season friendly match in Belgium.

He did, however, come back and played in one of the most memorable Easter Road matches. When Hibs beat Celtic 4–1 in February 1950 the match was noted for two things: firstly Eddie Turnbull scored all four Hibs goals (three of them were penalties) and secondly Clark played most of the game in

goal, having taken over from Tommy Younger when the score was only 1–1. Remarkably that was Clark's only appearance of the season!

A left-back, he spent two seasons with St Johnstone in the mid-1950s.

Appearances: 17 Goals: 1

COLGAN Nick

An Irish goalkeeper, Nick was signed by Alex McLeish and joined Hibs on the eve of their return to the Premier League in the wake of Bryan Gunn's serious injury.

Born in Drogheda, he worked hard to win over a rather sceptical Hibs support. Week by week he improved and his shot stopping in the 2002/03 season finally cemented his place in the list of excellent Hibernian goalkeepers. Indeed, his prowess was sufficient to earn him a place in the Republic of Ireland squad.

Signed from Bournemouth, after a top-class apprenticeship at Chelsea, Nick made his debut in a CIS tie at Clyde in August 1999. A very approachable player off the field, Nick had an ability to relate to the fans. Occasionally he displayed a wonderful temper that would see him hoof the ball clean out of Easter Road in a rage, most notably against Hearts when he conceded a last minute penalty to Ricardo Fuller. He was sent off in the aftermath and this gave his rival Tony Caig a run in Bobby Williamson's side.

During the 2003/04 season, as Hibs financial woes intensified, Colgan was firstly loaned to Stockport and then transferred to Barnsley.

Appearances: 121 Goals: 0

COLLINS Derek

Born in Glasgow in 1969, Derek joined Morton in 1987 from Renfrew Waverley and spent over a decade with the Greenock club before Alex McLeish signed him for Hibernian.

Ostensibly a full-back, he could also play in midfield. Derek was not long at Easter Road

Above: *Nick Colgan.*

Right: *Derek Collins.*

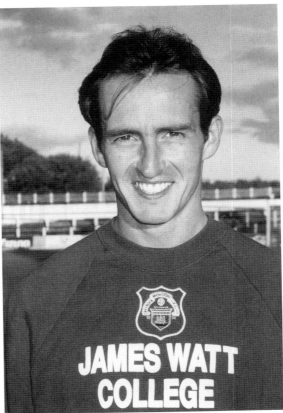

but did score a quite magnificent Scottish Cup goal against Dunfermline during his spell. He moved on to Partick Thistle before returning to Morton.

An energetic full-back, Derek was a reliable player who kept himself extremely fit.
Appearances: 39 Goals: 0

COLLINS John

John joined Hibs as a youngster from Hutchison Vale Boys Club in 1984. A native of Galashiels, he quickly revealed himself to be a talented and stylish midfielder. His debut came when aged just sixteen in a pre-season match against Manchester City and when he made his League bow, against Aberdeen, he was only a year older.

Hibernian were fortunate to acquire the services of the youthful Collins. By rights he should have joined Celtic, but the Glasgow club refused to pay John's travel expenses and thus he came to join Hibernian. In due course, paying a bus fare to and from Galashiels would earn the Hibees a cool £1 million.

With his cultured left foot, drive and dedication to improving he was the perfect young professional and Hibernian benefited greatly from his input. He earned his first Scotland cap while at Hibernian (making a scoring debut against Saudi Arabia in Riyadh in 1988).

In July 1990 he joined Celtic in a £1 million deal and six years later he travelled to France to join Monaco. He did not look out of place in what was rapidly becoming a very cultured league, the more studied nature of the game suiting his maturing style. What's more, his philosophy of improving his upper body strength began to reap dividends and he allied his cutting passes to an enormous strength on the ball.

He became a mainstay of the Scotland international side and had the joy of scoring the a goal in the 1998 World Cup finals as Scotland briefly threatened the mighty Brazil in the opening game of the tournament.

As his career wound down he played in England with Everton and Fulham.
Appearances: 163 Goals: 15

COMBE Bobby

One of the stars in the immediate post-war era, Bobby was signed in 1941 from Inveresk Thistle. Born less than a mile from Easter Road, he was persuaded to Hibernian by Willie McCartney when only seventeen years old and was audaciously snatched from under the noses of Hearts with whom he had been training.

In truth Bobby's debut was an historic occasion in the story of Hibernian. Also making his debut that day was one Gordon Smith and while Combe's single goal was excellent, Smith chipped in with a hat-trick

Bobby Combe.

John Collins.

that heralded the dawning of a new era at Easter Road.

Back to James Robert Combe. He was the epitome of the 'old head on young shoulders' and, shortly after his scoring debut against Hearts at Tynecastle, grabbed headlines that put even Smith in the shade! His remarkable feat was to bag four in the 8–1 demolition of Rangers. Indeed, in season 1941/42 he tallied an astonishing 27 goals, a sensational haul for an inside forward who had a liking for playing deep.

Around this time the Summer Cup was on its way to Easter Road. Given that Rangers were beaten in a thrilling final against the odds, Bobby Combe, who was a key part of that side, could be pleased with his early Easter Road endeavours.

Bobby built well on his notable start and was capped three times by Scotland as a half-back (against England, Belgium and Switzerland in 1948) and three times by the Scottish League.

The tag 'versatile' is often overused in football but in Bobby's case it is highly appropriate. One example proves the case perfectly. Lawrie Reilly missed only one game in the 1952/53 season. The occasion was a February fixture at Airdrie and many wondered how Hibs would cope with the disruption. Any worries were unfounded. Bobby Combe, who never missed a game that season himself, moved up from half-back to centre forward and scored four times in a powerful 7–3 victory.

Bobby stayed with Hibs until retiring at the end of the 1956/57 season. He won three League Championship medals while at Easter Road and at one stage was club captain. In both 1949/50 and 1952/53 he was an ever-present in League fixtures. Probably the low point of his time at Easter Road was the League Cup final defeat to Motherwell in 1951 when a side crammed with talented players froze on the big day.

In 1959 Bobby spent a short time in charge of Dumbarton before he began working with the Gas Board.
Appearances: 264 Goals: 54

CONNOLLY John

A superb young striker with St Johnstone and then Everton, John came to Hibernian in the twilight of his career. He stayed for fifteen months and played a key role in our First Division promotion in 1981.

All told his 49 outings brought 8 goals, which was no mean return for a veteran forward who liked to play tucked in behind a traditional centre forward. Several years later John's name came to prominence in the Scottish game when, as manager, he rekindled the fortunes of Queen of the South. By 2004 he was manager of St Johnstone.

John was born in Barrhead in 1950 and he won Scotland Under-23 caps while with Saints (whom he joined from Glasgow United) before leaving for Everton in a £70,000 deal in March 1972. Everton beat off stiff challenges from Rangers and Aberdeen for Connolly's services.
Appearances: 34 Goals: 8

CONROY Mike

Between 1982 and 1984 Mike played in 31 matches. His first senior goal for Hibs came against Kilmarnock in a 2–0 win at Rugby Park. Mike scored a couple of League Cup goals and a League goal in the 1983/84 season before moving on to Blackpool where he played 66 games. He later served both Wrexham and Leyton Orient.
Appearances: 31 Goals: 2

COOPER Neil

A composed and fairly constructive central defender, Neil joined Hibs in August 1989 from St Mirren for £30,000. His initial impact was to lend a degree of experience to the Hibernian defence.

He eventually lost out to the central defensive pairing of Hunter and McIntyre and moved to Aberdeen (his first senior club) for £20,000 in September 1991.

Neil was born in Aberdeen in 1959 and started his career at Pittodrie. Unable to dislodge Willie Miller from the side he moved to Barnsley in January 1980 for £35,000 and played at Oakwell and Grimsby Town before moving to St Mirren. He played in the UEFA Cup for St Mirren in season 1985/86.

Keen on coaching, Neil later managed Forfar Athletic.

Appearances: 38 Goals: 0

CORMACK Peter

Peter joined Hibs as a sixteen-year-old straight from Tynecastle Boys Club. He stayed for eight years and made the inside forward role his own. Skilful, energetic and creative, he thoroughly endeared himself to the Hibs faithful. Fiercely competitive, he fell foul of several referees (he was sent off four times as a Hibee) and was always capable of brightening up the dullest afternoon.

Peter made his Hibs debut against Airdrie at Broomfield in November 1962 and scored. At seventeen he played and scored for Hibs against the mighty Real Madrid – arguably the most famous football team in the world.

That cemented his place at Hibs and thereafter he developed into a solid inside forward who had enough skill and drive to stand out from the crowd. He could also turn his hand to goalkeeping and twice (against St Mirren and Hearts) deputised for the injured Willie Wilson. Capped against Brazil in 1966, it was the first of 9 caps he would win. His international career had begun with an Under-23 award while a Hibee and he scored in a 3–1 victory over England in 1967 (Pat Stanton was also in the victorious Scottish side).

Sadly the bulk of his caps were won while he was away from Easter Road. A precocious

Peter Cormack.

talent it was never likely that Hibernian would be able to hold him indefinitely and a switch to English football was a natural progression.

Cormack adapted well to life at Nottingham Forest, whom he joined in March 1970, and was soon on his way to Liverpool. The honours simply cascaded into the Cormack display cabinet and his time at Anfield saw him win two Championships, two UEFA Cups and an FA Cup.

He had a second spell at Hibs before beginning a coaching career that saw him work at Partick, in Cyprus and at Morton and Cowdenbeath.

Appearances: 200 Goals: 77

COUSIN Alan

A tall, vastly experienced wing-back, Alan was signed for Hibs by Bob Shankly in 1965. Shankly had been Cousin's manager at Dens when the Dark Blues landed the 1962 League Championship.

He was by no means an ordinary 'run of the mill' footballer. He was a Latin and Greek scholar, had graduated from St Andrew's

Steve Cowan.

University and would frequently travel to away games devouring classical texts.

He was a part-time player with Hibs too, teaching classics in an Alloa school, but still displayed enough class to be a valuable team member.

Appearances: 84 Goals: 2

COWAN Steve

His career had started with St Mirren under Alex Ferguson. He followed Fergie to Aberdeen where he was a fringe striker, before moving to Hibernian in 1985 where the goals arrived thick and fast.

He had three hat-tricks in his first season at Hibs, and helped the club reach both the League and Scottish Cup semi-finals. With 19 goals from 36 League matches he had certainly made a mark. Sadly he only managed four goals in the next term and was moved on to Motherwell. He later starred in Irish football and Portadown were among those to benefit from his goalscoring prowess.

Appearances: 70 Goals: 23

CRAIG Tommy

Signed in the winter of 1984 from Carlisle United, Tommy was a midfield schemer who had, in all fairness, probably played his best football at the likes of Sheffield Wednesday and Wolves before joining Hibernian.

Nevertheless he gave a calm and assured performance in his debut, which came in a derby against Hearts.

After a short spell playing for Hibs he began a coaching career that took in stints with several clubs.

Appearances: 11 Goals: 0

CRAWFORD Stevie

A lithe, intricate forward, Stevie made the short trip from Rosyth Recreation to Raith Rovers and promptly scored in the Fife derby against Dunfermline.

He won promotions and League Cup medals, as well as his first Scotland cap, with Raith before joining Millwall. Jimmy Nicholl bossed Millwall at the time and the genial Irishman had been Crawford's manager for most of his career at Raith Rovers.

Although a prolific marksman for the London side he soon found himself to be an asset in a side that was financially strapped. He duly signed for Hibs for £400,000.

His 12 goals in the First Division campaign were vital to the club's promotion and his speedy play and clever distribution made him a very popular player. He moved to Dunfermline in February 1999 and proved a most able striker for the Pars. Indeed, in 2003 he returned to Easter Road with his new club and scored in a Scottish Cup replay, which Hibs lost 0–2. He was a major part of the Dunfermline scene until 2004 when he joined Plymouth under Bobby Williamson. In 2005

Steve Crawford.

43

he returned homesick to Scotland and Dundee United before moving on again in the summer of that year, this time to Aberdeen.
Appearances: 71 Goals: 23

CROPLEY Alex

Born in Aldershot in January 1951, Alexander James Cropley was one of the key elements of the famous Turnbull's Tornadoes side. A gifted, slight and crafty inside forward he burst into the team in the 1968/69 season and by the early 1970s was an integral part of the Hibernian set-up.

Alex made his debut against St Mirren in March 1969 and for a couple of seasons flitted in and out of the first team from the sidelines. He served notice of his talent on the opening day of the 1971 season when he scored against Hearts in a 2–0 win at Tynecastle and he repeated his derby goalscoring exploits some two years later when he scored in the 7–0 massacre. Clearly he enjoyed the capital clashes for he also scored twice when we beat Hearts 3–1 in January 1974.

While with Hibs Alex won a League Cup badge and played in a Scottish Cup final. He was also part of the side that reached the 1975 League Cup final and was capped by Scotland at Under-23 level, before playing twice for the full international side.

Alas, others noted his talents too and in 1974 he moved to Arsenal for £150,000. It was perhaps a rather unfortunate time to join the North London giants for, unusually, they were languishing in the relegation zone at the time. After 34 games for the Gunners he joined Aston Villa in 1976 for £125,000 and won a League Cup medal.
Appearances: 125 Goals: 29

CUTHBERT Ian

Ian was registered with Hibs as an amateur on 5 July 1960. He then signed professional terms on 9 January 1961. Season 1961/62 saw him make his only outing for the club and he was released at the end of the 1962/63 campaign.
Appearances: 1 Goals: 0

CUTHBERTSON Johnny

A 1939 signing from Ayrshire junior side Craigmark, Johnny 'Cubby' Cuthbertson became a Hibernian hero with his dashing forward play. He burst into the first team in the 1946/47 season and bagged five goals in only nine League starts.

The high point of his Hibs' career was surely scoring the opening goal in the 1947 Scottish Cup final against Aberdeen. This early goal was timed at just 30 seconds but Hibernian faltered after the brightest of starts and eventually lost the match 1–2. Cubby had more joy with a late goal in the 1947/48 season when he bagged a last minute winner in a 1–0 win over Rangers at Easter Road – a goal incidentally netted before a crowd of 53,000, which constituted a Hibs record at the time.

He was frustrated by a lack of first-team openings in a very strong Hibernian side and moved to Third Lanark in July 1949. He was a sensation at Third Lanark with his total application, wonderful ball control and trigger-happy style and bagged 55 goals for the Cathkin side from just 103 games.

After hanging up his boots Johnny Cuthbertson worked as a civil servant and completed his service in the heart of Yorkshire at Wetherby.

One lovely story surrounding Cuthbertson concerns teammate Ally MacLeod's mother. Ally's mum was so taken with Johnny that she named her cat after him – Cubby.

Reference is often made to Cuthbertson's dramatic early goal in the 1947 Scottish Cup final. However, less well known is the fact that in the very next Scottish Cup Hibernian ended up playing Aberdeen in the third round. Lo and behold, despite being well

Alex Cropley.

warned, Aberdeen conceded a goal after only 20 seconds to… Cuthbertson!
Appearances: 33 Goals: 29

D

D'ARCY Tommy
A centre forward, he was signed in 1952 from Armadale Thistle. He made three League outings in 1953/54 but enjoyed much more success in the League Cup, scoring several goals including a hat-trick. However, he could not settle at Easter Road and in September 1954 moved to Bournemouth. Alas, he did not fit in there either and returned to Hibs only to move to Southend in the summer of 1956. His career ended with a short stint at Queen of the South.
Appearances: 3 Goals: 0

DACQUIN Frederic

One of Alex McLeish's brace of young French signings, Frederic was signed from Paris St Germaine but failed to live up to high expectations. There was a brief run in the team during the summer of 2002 but it amounted to only two games and soon he was on his way back to France.

Appearances: 4 Goals: 0

DAVIDSON Kenny

Signed in August 1970, Kenny had to overcome a compound leg-fracture to make his mark with Hibernian. A talented winger, his debut was memorable in that it came in a Fairs Cup tie against Mälmo.

His first goals came early in the 1970/71 season when he bagged a brace against St Mirren. He had another two in a Scottish Cup win over Forfar and was an established part of the first-team pool by the end of that season with 4 goals in 11 League matches. However he managed only a handful of games the following season and as a left-winger lost out to the more experienced Arthur Duncan.

Appearances: 15 Goals: 4

DAVIN Joe

Born in Dumbarton in 1942, Joe played 16 matches for Hibs between 1959 and 1963 without ever being a regular. He moved to Ipswich in July 1963 and went on to make 77 outings in two seasons for the Suffolk club. He was a full-back and returned to Scotland to serve Morton and Dumbarton briefly.

Appearances: 16 Goals: 0

DAVIS Joe

Signed from Third Lanark in November 1964, it is doubtful if Hibs have ever had a more prolific goalscorer from defence. He netted his first goal for Hibs in a League Cup tie against Alloa in September 1965 and by August 1967 had 31 goals to his name!

Joe Davis.

Joe turned senior with Third Lanark, whom he joined from Shettleston Juniors in February 1961. Third's historian Bert Bell points out that: 'Joe was part of the famous Hi-Hi side that won the Glasgow Cup in 1964; an occasion notable for the fact that it was the last ever trophy triumph for Thirds.'

An energetic player, he was well capable of both snuffing out and generating attacking moves. It was however as a goal scoring full-back that he earned real fame. The bulk of his goals came from the penalty mark; indeed, at one stage he converted 29 out of 34 spot kicks (sadly of his infrequent misses two came in derbies against Hearts). In short, Davis was remarkably consistent and he is credited with an astonishing run of 273 consecutive games for Hibernian.

It was only the arrival of manager Willie MacFarlane that signalled an end to 'the Davis period'. Willie came from Stirling Albion and quickly returned to that club to sign left-back Erich Schaedler. Given that Hibs also had Chris Shevlane, Mervyn Jones and Willie

McEwan on the books, the openings for Joe were decreasing. He stayed at Easter Road until December 1969 when the opportunity to move to England arose.

It was Carlisle United who offered him the chance to sample the English League and he was with the Cumbrians for two seasons in which time he played 79 League games. He did not score for United, however, which rather suggests they had another penalty taker!
Appearances: 157 Goals: 34

DEITRICH Klaus

A former Austrian Under-21 international, Klaus joined Hibs when the club were in the First Division under Alex McLeish. A central defender, he stayed very briefly having joined the club from GAK Graz. He played a single competitive match for Hibs, a shock 2–0 defeat at Love Street against St Mirren. Ironically enough he also played once for Saints early in the 2002/03 season.
Appearances: 1 Goals: 0

DE LA CRUZ Ulises

Born in Ecuador in 1974, Ulises was an Ecuadorian international with over 50 caps when Hibernian made him their record signing the summer of 2001. He made a huge impact with his surging runs and clever use of the ball. His golden day came in the October 2001 Hibernian-Hearts derby at Easter Road when he scored both Hibs goals in a 2–1 win, including a quite stunning first minute opener.

Ulises played for Ecuador in the Japan/Korea World Cup finals in 2002 and was arguably his nation's finest player. This was sufficient to earn him a big-money move to Aston Villa upon his return to Britain in July 2002.
Appearances: 32 Goals: 2

DEMPSIE Alan

Broke into the first team during Bobby Williamson's reign. Brother of Mark he was a quick and decisive and had three games at the end of the 2001/02 season. However, he was unable to establish himself thereafter.
Appearances: 5 Goals: 0

DEMPSIE Mark

A central defender, Mark made his debut in 1999 against St Mirren. Given that Hibs won the match despite playing much of it with ten men it was an impressive bow. It is ironic then that he should move from Hibs to St Mirren in January 2003.

Mark had been linked with Hibs from the age of nine when Martin Ferguson lured him to the club. It was Jim Duffy who signed him officially. Sadly, he was plagued by injury and this hampered his progress. He also had the misfortune to play in the middle of the defence that lost 5–1 to Hearts at Tynecastle Park in 2002.
Appearances: 20 Goals: 0

Ulises De La Cruz.

Shaun Dennis.

DENNIS Shaun

A towering central defender, Shaun had been a mining apprentice when Raith Rovers offered him an escape into football. He seized it with both hands and gave Rovers seven years' excellent service before moving to Hibs in January 1997. As part of that deal Andy Millen moved to Raith.

A colossus of a man, Dennis was a hard but fair defender who lacked nothing in bravery. He could also score the odd goal but in truth lacked that wee touch of pace to hit the heights.

Dennis eventually returned to Rovers having won First Division Championship medals with both Hibs and Raith, but importantly having won a League Cup badge in his time as a Rover.

Appearances: 63 Goals: 4

DOBBIE Stephen

Scored a first-half CIS hat-trick when Hibs beat Montrose 9–0 and then bagged the vital equaliser in the epic penalty shootout win over Rangers in the semi-finals – thus Stephen quickly became a popular Hibee. Stephen joined Hibs from Rangers in May 2003 and, despite being hampered by injury, had scored 14 goals for Rangers Under-21s in the term he moved. Nippy and packing a powerful shot he was a lively forward whom both Bobby Williamson and Tony Mowbray liked to utilise from the bench.

Appearances: 28 Goals: 2

DOCHERTY Peter

A young forward who made his bow in the 1979/80 relegation season. He was a substitute in the final game of that ill-fated term, which, rather fittingly, Hibs lost 1–0 at home to Partick Thistle.

Appearances: 3 Goals: 0

DODS Darren

Born in Edinburgh in 1975, Darren joined Hibs in August 1992 from Hutcheson Vale BC.

Darren Dods.

After impressing in the youth system, and helping the club win the BP Youth Cup, he made his full debut in May 1995 against Kilmarnock and in the following two seasons edged his way further into the first-team picture. However, his progress was hampered by a temper and occasional clumsiness that saw him sent off against Celtic and Kilmarnock in rapid succession.

Despite winning five Scotland Under-21 caps and displaying enormous enthusiasm and will to win he could never quite make himself an automatic selection. With that in mind he moved on to St Johnstone in the summer of 1998.

Appearances: 65 Goals: 1

DONALD Graeme

A very versatile youngster, Graeme joined Hibs in 1991 and was soon breaking into the first team. In his first season he scored three goals in just five games and a promising career beckoned.

What went wrong is hard to identify. He gained Scotland Under-21 caps and made over thirty outings for Hibs but was never quite an automatic selection.

He later moved on to Stirling Albion and Stenhousemuir.

Appearances: 52 Goals: 5

DOUMBE Matthias

Born in Rancy, a village near Lyon in France, Mathias started his senior career with Paris St Germaine. It was from the French giants that Alex McLeish signed him for Hibs.

He made his debut against Rangers in August 2002 and, although it was a tentative start, he eventually broke into the team as a regular. Athletic, talented and very composed he settled well to his task and seemed to gain in confidence when playing alongside Colin Murdock, who was extremely encouraging.

In the summer of 2004 he followed manager Bobby Williamson to Plymouth Argyle.

Appearances: 46 Goals: 2

DOW Andy

Signed from Chelsea for £125,000 in 1996, Dow, an industrious and busy player, made an instant impact. A former Scotland Under-21 cap, Andy had both pace and strength, key assets for a full-back in the modern game.

Prior to joining Chelsea he had played with Dundee and Bradford City. He left Hibs in 1998 after two and half years in Edinburgh to join his former boss Alex Miller at Aberdeen. This departure was more a reflection on Hibs' financial status at the time than a comment on his usefulness to the Hibs cause. Stints with Motherwell and St Mirren were also squeezed in before his senior career ended

Appearances: 62 Goals: 3

DUCHART Alex

Born in Falkirk in May 1933, Alex spent the early part of his career at Easter Road, having starred for Falkirk in a trial at Hibernian! He played three times in the 1953/54 season. In May 1956 he left Hibs to join Southend United in England but within a few years was back in Scotland with Falkirk, with whom he won promotion in 1961.

Appearances: 3 Goals: 0

DUNCAN Arthur

Capped 6 times by Scotland and playing in 448 League games for Hibs it is clear that Arthur is one of the most noted Hibernian players of the modern era.

Arthur joined Partick Thistle straight from school and his Jags debut is a memorable story. The experienced and rather robust Alex Hamilton of Dundee was his direct opponent and handed the young Duncan a complimentary stand ticket. It came with the advice: 'use this son, because you will not get a kick of the ball today'.

Fortunately Arthur was not put off by such gamesmanship and by December 1969 had made sufficient progress to convince Hibs boss Willie MacFarlane to sign him. To have picked

Arthur Duncan.

up such a talented outside left for a mere £35,000 has to be viewed as a supreme bargain.

A flying winger, Arthur quickly won over the Hibs support who dubbed him 'Nijinski' after the super fast racehorse of that name. Duncan played in many memorable matches but had the misfortune to score the decisive own goal when Hibs lost the Scottish Cup final replay to Rangers in 1979.

Something of a fitness fanatic, Arthur's 6 Scotland caps were gained in a 114-day period in 1975 with Willie Ormond being the Scotland boss at the time. Ormond, like Duncan, had been a left-wing darling of the Easter Road slopes.

Arthur Duncan's career at Hibs ended in an historical fashion. He broke his collarbone in an East of Scotland Shield match against Meadowbank Thistle and this incident helped end the practice of first-team players playing in the competition. Thereafter it became a tournament reserved for youth and fringe players.

After leaving Hibs Arthur played with Meadowbank before concentrating on being a full time chiropodist. Throughout his time at Easter Road he had worked part time for the Central Regional Health Board and their predecessors.

My good friend Stuart Crowther told me the best story concerning the wonderful career of Arthur Duncan. Stuart's brother was serving in the army in Germany at the time of the Hibs *v.* Rangers 1979 Scottish Cup final replay. On patrol that night he was unable to tune into the game and relied on colleagues to keep him informed of the scoring. He could barely contain his excitement but then came the news of the final result from a colleague: '… it's finished 3–2'.

'Who for?' asked the near hysterical young Crowther.

'I don't know,' replied the squaddie. 'But some guy called Arthur Duncan scored the winner.'

Cue major celebrations amongst Clan Crowther and a night of sheer bliss as the cup hoodoo was shattered.

Imagine therefore the emotional devastation the following morning when newspapers revealed that while Arthur had indeed scored the crucial goal… it had been an own goal!
Appearances: 448 Goals: 73

DUNCAN Bobby

It was from Bonnyrigg Rose in 1961 that Hibs signed the then young inside forward. However, he was quickly converted to a full-back and it is in that position that he made the majority of his Hibernian appearances.

He did well to recover from a broken leg sustained against Celtic in 1968 and was a regular with East Fife in the early 1970s, wracking up 85 appearances in just three seasons in Methil.
Appearances: 74 Goals: 0

DURIE Gordon

A magnificent striker, Gordon joined Hibs from East Fife and proved to be John Blackley's finest signing for the club. The only pity was that Gordon Durie was not a Hibernian player for nearly long enough.

Although born in Paisley he was brought up in Fife and played his early football with Hill of Beath. He graduated to senior football with East Fife in 1981 and quickly proved able to hold his own in the Second Division, helping the Fifers gain promotion in 1984 with a haul of 16 goals in 32 League starts.

But for Hibernian supporters the abiding memory is of a humbling Scottish Cup exit we suffered at Bayview. The die was cast and John Blackley convinced the Hibs board to allow him to spend £70,000 in signing Durie.

He settled superbly at Easter Road and his strong, forceful style quickly cemented his place in the fans' affections. He scored two

Gordon Durie.

goals in two minutes to ensure a vital relegation win over Dumbarton and a hat-trick against Morton in February 1985 confirmed his quality. Indeed, with Willie Irvine absent through injury, Gordon's prowess was absolutely vital.

As the 1985/86 season unfolded it was clear that it would be hard to hang on to Gordon Durie. He linked well with Stevie Cowan and helped the club reach the 1985 League Cup final by scoring in the 2–0 semi-final first leg win over Rangers. Moreover, he had netted a hat-trick in the 6–1 quarter-final win over Motherwell. Hibs also reached the semi-finals of the Scottish Cup that season, again falling to Aberdeen, but many reckon the fielding of Durie as a midfielder rather than a striker fatally hindered the semi-final cause.

In April 1986 Gordon joined Chelsea for around £400,000. He was a huge success at Stamford Bridge and later played with distinction for Tottenham Hotspur and then Rangers, for whom he scored a hat-trick in the 1996 Scottish Cup final rout of Hearts.

Eventually Gordon returned to Edinburgh – but in the colours of Hearts. He did manage to come back to Easter Road but will probably want to forget the occasion as Hibs thumped their great rivals 6–2.

Throughout his career Gordon took enormous pride in representing Scotland and his total of 33 caps in what was an injury-ravaged career is impressive. What a shame he did not spend more of his career at Easter Road. *Appearances: 47 Goals: 14*

E

EASTON Jim

A centre half, Jim was signed from Drumchapel Amateurs in 1959. Strong in the tackle he was a good organiser and between 1960 and 1964 was a regular in the Hibs defence.

He was sold to Dundee in October 1964 and enjoyed just over six solid seasons there before moving on to Queen of the South. In 1973 he tried his luck in America with Miami. *Appearances: 79 Goals: 1*

EDGE Roland

A left wing-back, Roland was signed by Bobby Williamson in 2003 from Gillingham. He played for Hibs in the 2004 CIS Cup final against Livingston but in truth he took time to find his feet at Easter Road and he left the club shortly after Williamson himself had moved to Plymouth. Roland's destination was the rather less salubrious Hull. *Appearances: 20 Goals: 0*

EDWARDS Alex

Alex Edwards joined Dunfermline when he was fifteen and made his debut at that tender age against Hibernian. Clearly he made an impression because the Pars ran out 4–0 victors.

Edwards excelled with Dunfermline, winning a Scottish Cup medal (against Hearts) in 1968, featuring in several high-profile European matches and picking up Scottish League and Under-23 awards.

He had his admirers at Easter Road from an early stage. Indeed, the Hibs match programme for the fixture with Dunfermline in August 1969 said of him: 'The principal schemer for the visitors is little Alex Edwards who passes a good ball and teases goalkeepers with his cleverly flighted crosses. He was switched from the orthodox right-wing role to midfield last season and Alex enjoys being more in the game.' The success of that switch probably convinced Hibernian to make their move.

Hibs signed Alex when he was twenty-five and picked up a real bargain at £13,000. The Hibs price, however, was slightly compromised in that Alex was actually serving one of his many suspensions at the time! Indeed, there was a five-week 'sentence' to serve before he could make his debut.

Under Turnbull Edwards thrived and won a League Cup winner's medal and Dryburgh Cup badges. Alex also built upon the European experience he had gained at Dunfermline. While with Hibs he regularly featured on the European stage but it was against English opposition that he gave one of his best showings. The match was a UEFA Cup tie against Liverpool in 1975 and Edwards had the Hibs counter in the 3–1 reversal at Anfield that saw Hibs bow out narrowly 2–3 on aggregate.

Just what kind of player was Edwards? It is probably fair to say that he was a midfield dynamo. He had a good engine, was not afraid to graft and tended to create openings for those around him.

Aged thirty-two he finally left Hibs and joined Arbroath briefly before retiring from the game. When he gave up football he concentrated on his farmhouse in Fife and became extremely interested in horses.
Appearances: 142 Goals: 5

ELLIOT David

David began his senior career with Celtic but like many youngsters struggled to gain regular football. He therefore moved in rapid fashion to Partick Thistle, St Mirren and Falkirk.

It was Jim Duffy who took David to Hibs in January 1997 and he featured fairly regularly until Alex McLeish arrived. Although he played sporadically with Alex at the helm his Easter Road career was drawing to a close and he played only eight games in the promotion-winning season before moving on.
Appearances: 19 Goals: 0

Alex Edwards.

EVANS Gareth

Signed in February 1988 from Rotherham United Gareth made the conversion from English Third Division football to the Scottish Premier League with ease. He scored on his debut against Dundee but took time to settle and at one stage was keen to return to England. So keen indeed that he welcomed loan spells with Stoke City and Northampton Town.

A League Cup winner in 1991, Gareth's confidence seemed to soar thereafter and with his electric pace and busy manner he was a handful for defences. A consistent performer he matured as a player and gradually became more methodical in his approach.

Supremely fit, he seldom missed matches through injury and, when he curbed his temper, he was a regular fixture in the side for several years. After leaving Hibs he played with Partick Thistle, Airdrie and Alloa. He even contrived to get sent off against Hibs while with Airdrie!

Appearances: 247 Goals: 29

Gareth Evans.

F

FALCONER Duncan

Signed from Edinburgh Norton in 1959, this strong inside forward was just under six feet tall and able to use his physique to good advantage. Nevertheless, he made a slow start to a Hibs career that proved somewhat stop-start in nature.

In the 1959/60 season he made his breakthrough into the first team but 10 games produced no goals. Such a return ensured that he only played in 5 League fixtures the next campaign but, quite surprisingly, he topped the Hibernian scoring charts in the 1961/62 season, grabbing 12 League counters.

It proved a false dawn. Over the next couple of seasons he barely managed to add to that total, although he did enjoy hitting the winner in a Fairs Cup tie against Utrecht.

Not surprisingly his Hibs career somewhat fizzled out. After playing with Hibernian he emigrated to Australia but returned to Britain in order to join the police force in Tunbridge Wells.

Appearances: 48 Goals: 14

FARM George

A 1947 signing from Armadale Thistle, George was a fine goalkeeper who would eventually become an equally fine manager.

Born in Slateford in 1924, he played in seven matches in the championship-winning side of 1947/48. In September 1948 he headed for the bright lights of Blackpool, then a major force in the English game. While there he kept goal for Scotland 10 times, most notably at Wembley in a 4–1 defeat but earned more fame as a Blackpool regular making a staggering 462 appearances between 1948 and 1959.

From Blackpool he returned to Scotland to keep goal for Queen of the South but it was

as manager of Dunfermline Athletic that he made his biggest impression.
Appearances: 7 Goals: 0

FARMER Jim

A full-back, Jim joined Hibs in the late 1970s and played a handful of games. He hailed from the Stenhouse district of Edinburgh.
Appearances: 4 Goals: 0

FARRELL David

Signed as a nineteen-year-old in December 1988 from Oxford United, he was a gritty mid-fielder. David stayed at Hibernian for a few years and was something of a mainstay in the side of 1993/94. That was fortuitous timing as Hibernian reached the League Cup final in October and David played his part that day.

A Scotland Under-18 cap he had made his Hibs debut against Aberdeen in 1990 but rather flitted in and out of the team before and after the 1993/94 campaign. When he moved on he had amassed 110 League outings in his six years at Easter Road. He later played with Partick Thistle before spending a short time with Airdrie.
Appearances: 110 Goals: 2

FELLENGER David

John Blackley signed David as a sixteen-year-old from Hutcheson Vale BC, despite the attentions of Hearts, Dundee United and East Fife, he made his debut in the 1988/89 season against Aberdeen in a League Cup tie. Over the following two seasons the Edinburgh-born forward began to increase his presence in the first team but a complicated broken leg in 1992 virtually ended his Hibs career.
Appearances: 46 Goals: 4

FENWICK Paul

Recruited in the summer of 2000, Paul made his debut in the torrid atmosphere of an

Paul Fenwick.

Edinburgh derby in July of that year. The big Canadian international had won a Gold Cup medal in 1999 and played with Birmingham, Dunfermline, St Mirren, Morton and Raith in a career that steadily improved.

When playing alongside the likes of Franck Sauzee and Ulrik Laursen he more than proved his worth. Sadly he lost his place at Easter Road when the club undertook a cost-cutting exercise that meant Paul was simply too expensive to play. He stayed on at Hibs, seeing out his contract but not playing first-team football.
Appearances: 84 Goals: 4

FINDLAY Billy

Born in Kilmarnock, Billy joined Hibs from Killie Boys Club and in truth made a bigger impression when returning to Kilmarnock than he had with Hibs. Like several Hibs players at that time who showed promise he was a Scotland Under-21 international.

When Billy moved to Kilmarnock, it was in a swap-deal for Andy Millen. From Killie it was on to Ayr United and he scored a vital goal for them, saving their First Division status at the expense of Partick Thistle in a 'do-or-die' clash at Firhill. Later in his career Billy joined Queen of the South, Sligo Rovers, Kilwinning Rangers and Maybole Juniors.
Appearances: 119 Goals: 7

FINNEGAN Willie

Recruited in 1937 from Bo'ness Cadera, Willie had twice represented Scotland Juniors before coming to Easter Road.

A hard running half-back or inside forward, his finest hour arrived when he helped Hibs win the Summer Cup, scoring twice in the 3–2 final win over Rangers. His career was badly disrupted by the hostilities. However, he did play in 18 matches in the first full season following the Second World War. He had eight games the very next season but was slipping from the picture and Dunfermline signed Willie in July 1950.

Of his time at Easter Road he told one lovely story concerning an away match. Trooping off the field after a 1–0 win for Hibs he heard the disconsolate home goalkeeper remark to his teammates: 'Well at least that's one of my aways up!'
Appearances: 41 Goals: 1

FLAVELL Bobby

Born in Berwick in March 1956, Flavell had played with Bonnyrigg Boys Club before embarking on a fairly nomadic career.

From school he went to Burnley before Halifax Town, Chesterfield and Barnsley utilised his midfield talents. He was with Swedish side Vastar Haninge in 1981 when Bertie Auld signed him for Hibs. He made his debut as a full-back but soon reverted to midfield duties.

He netted at Ibrox in a 1–1 draw and was a regular in the 1981/82 season. But he played just four games the next season before moving to Motherwell in the deal that brought Willie Irvine to Easter Road.

After Motherwell there was time to savour the delights of Dundee United and Berwick Rangers before retiring from the game.
Appearances: 36 Goals: 2

FLEMING Rikki

Signed from Ayr United in 1978 for £10,000, Rikki had once been on the books of Rangers. He was a commanding centre-back for the Honest Men, spending a decade at Somerset Park following his November 1968 transfer from Kilwinning Rangers, and it was hoped he would provide similar solidity for Hibs.

He never quite hit it off with Hibs and his stay was a short one. Rikki played just a dozen games in the 1978/79 campaign before he was off. His debut came against Dundee United at Tannadice and away from football he retained an interest in pursuing his trade as a boiler-maker.

By the start of the 1979/80 season Rikki had joined Berwick Rangers.
Appearances: 12 Goals: 0

FLETCHER Steven

A young striker who came through the Hibernian youth system and broke into the first team at the tail end of the 2003/04 season, making his debut against Livingston. A Scotland Under-19 international, the club has high hopes for him.
Appearances: 5 Goals: 0

FOX Desmond

A centre forward, despite standing at only 5ft 5in, Desmond saw his early Hibernian career disrupted by National Service. For a while he was stationed in Cyprus but was later posted to Dover. He made the most of his situation there by playing for Dover Town.

He had joined Hibs in 1955 from Armadale Thistle. From that point until 1961 he was to play in 32 League fixtures, which brought him 8 goals. His first goal for the club came in a sectional League Cup tie against Dunfermline Athletic. In February 1960 he joined the Pars great rivals – Raith Rovers.

Appearances: 32 Goals: 8

FRANKS Mike

A 6ft 5in goalkeeper, Mike joined Hibernian in the autumn of 2000 and made a quite dramatic debut. He came on for Nick Colgan during a 0–0 draw with Celtic when the Irishman sustained an injury. A quick save and he settled to the task.

Mike had been raised in Edmonton, Canada and his football career had taken him from Vancouver 86s to PSV Eindhoven. Capped by the Canadian Under-23 Olympic team, he played just one more game for Hibernian (the match against Motherwell that followed the Celtic game) before moving on.

Appearances: 2 Goals: 0

FRASER John

When John joined Hibernian in 1954 from Edinburgh Thistle there was considerable difficulty working out which was his best position. Listed as an outside right, he filled three forward positions in his first season. And what a first season it was too with three goals in just four outings!

A native of Portobello, he was initially on National Service when he came to Easter Road. Signed by Hugh Shaw, few could have guessed at the time that John would be part and parcel of the Hibs scene for some twenty-five years.

Given that his initial task was to replace the wonderful Gordon Smith, it would have been easy for John to give up, but he gradually established himself as a Hibernian favourite. In season 1956/57 he scored 9 times in just 20 starts and had the considerable pleasure of scoring one of the goals in a Ne'erday 2–0 win at Tynecastle.

Measuring 5ft 9in and bristling with enthusiasm, John did what many players have since done, moved from the forward line to a position further back. There he could use his uncanny knack of spotting danger before it reached crisis point and offer assistance to younger players further forward. His goals tended come in fits and starts but in 1961 he scored twice in a Fairs Cup tie against Belenenses.

At one stage in his career John was Hibs' captain, and that seems a fitting accolade for a very faithful player. He brought the curtain down on his playing days with a short spell at Stenhousemuir then returned to Hibs working as a coach under Shankly, MacFarlane and finally Turnbull.

Appearances: 195 Goals: 25

FRASER Robert

Played in five games during the 1946/47 season as normal football resumed. He had been signed on 3 September 1938. He was transferred to Newcastle United during the 1946/47 season.

Appearances: 5 Goals: 0

FRYE John

Rather unfortunate with injuries and illness while at Easter Road, John had scored in prestigious floodlit matches against Tottenham and Wolves before he suffered ligament damage in a match against St Mirren. His Easter Road impetus was lost and in a supreme irony he was sold to the Saints in March 1960.

He had joined Hibs as an outside right from Ardrossan Winton Rovers in 1955 and scored his first League goal in 1957 against Queen's Park at Hampden Park but in twenty League outings that was his only goal.

His son Derek was a professional with Stranraer, Dundee United, Ayr United and Clyde.

Appearances: 20 Goals: 1

FULTON Mark

A towering centre half, Mark was born in Johnstone in 1959 and played with the local Burgh junior side until 1977 when he joined St Mirren.

He was outstanding at the heart of the Paisley defence, collecting 5 Under-21 caps, until Hibs came calling. Joining Hibs for the 1985/86 season he made 30 Premier League appearances that term but played only nine games in the following campaign before moving to Hamilton Accies.

Appearances: 39 Goals: 0

FYFE Graham

In 1976 Hibs swapped the gifted Ian Munro for two fringe Rangers players: Ally Scott was one and Graham Fyfe the other. Fyfe had been a player who promised much at Ibrox but never quite established himself as an automatic selection despite playing in almost 100 matches. At Hibernian he could not force himself into the team. It was interesting that while with Rangers he had constantly menaced Hibernian and scored several goals against us.

Fyfe had joined Rangers from Ashfield Juniors and joined Hibs in his prime as a twenty-five-year-old. In total he played just 11 League games as a Hibee and it remains difficult to fathom out quite what went wrong for Graham in Edinburgh.

Appearances: 11 Goals: 1

G

GALLACHER Michael

Although born in Donegal, Michael joined Hibernian in 1946 from Alloa Athletic. He played 4 times in the 1948/49 season and by the 1951/52 season, when Hibs won the title, had upped his participation to 19 matches. Yet for all his efforts he was essentially a squad player.

He went to Ayr United in October 1954 along with Jock Govan, not long after being capped by Ireland against Luxembourg.

Gallacher made a great success of his move to Ayrshire. He played in 76 League matches for United, including all of those required for Ayr to win promotion in '55/56. Unfortunately he was injured the following season and in the summer of was granted a free transfer and moved to

After retiring from playing career emigrated America and ran a bar in Chicago death on 3 January 1984.

Appearances: 49 Goals: 0

GIBSON Davie

National Service duties disrupted Hibernian career of this powerful centre forward, who was born in Winchburgh in 1938. Signed from Livingston United in 1956, he was a clever player who used the ball very well and as his career progressed he proved a useful finisher too.

After making 41 League appearances between 1956 and 1962 he was sold to Leicester City in January of 1962. He had only scored 8 goals for Hibs in that time but he proved a most effective striker for City and bagged 41 goals in 280 League matches for the Foxes. He also played in an FA Cup final and won 7 full Scotland caps.

In the early 1960s, matches between an Edinburgh Select and English opposition

were a traditional curtain raiser to the season in Edinburgh and in one of the those matches Dave Gibson scored a hat-trick but still ended on the losing side. Burnley won the game 7–4 and two of their players netted hat-tricks!
Appearances: 41 Goals: 8

GLASS Stephen

Signed in the summer of 2003 from Watford, Stephen made his name in Scottish football as a youngster with Aberdeen. He then completed a big-money move to Newcastle United, where he played in an FA Cup final against Chelsea but generally failed to meet the levels expected. Thus he spent a season and a half with Watford, scoring a memorable FA up goal for the Hornets. A former Scotland Under-21 international, his career at Easter Road was initially a little stop-start due to a succ niggling injuries. By 2004 he was nder Tony Mowbray and had h ur ge the club in a 4–0 League up er Alloa at Easter Road.
s: 12 Goals: 0

Andy

the finest post-war goalkeeper to Scotland, Andy was born in Bury in and was the son of former Hibs 'keeper Lew Goram (who never played for the first team at Hibs but did play on loan for Leith Athletic).

From humble beginnings with Oldham Athletic (and selection for an England Under-21 squad), Andy moved to Hibs for £325,000 in October 1987. He was an instant success at Easter Road and in 1988 earned a special niche for himself by scoring from a kick-out against Morton. By 1990 he was in the Scotland squad travelling to Italy for the World Cup finals but, alas, a year later he was sold to Rangers for £1 million. He was an outstanding 'keeper for the Glasgow club too and won many, many honours while there.

Andy Goram.

He represented Scotland at cricket but was occasionally attracting newspaper headlines for the wrong reasons. In 1998 he was axed by Rangers and after stints with Sheffield United and Notts County joined Motherwell as John Boyle sought to make the Lanarkshire club 'the third force' in Scottish football.

In 2001 he sensationally joined Manchester United when the English Champions had an injury crisis. Flamboyant, controversial and a wonderful shot stopper, he was always an entertaining figure. As late as 2002 he was playing first-team football, albeit his debut for Oldham ending in a 1–7 defeat! By 2003 he had joined Queen of the South.
Appearances: 138 Goals: 1

GORDON Alan

It was Alan Gordon who extracted from an irritable Eddie Turnbull one of the all-time great football quotes. Annoyed at Gordon's

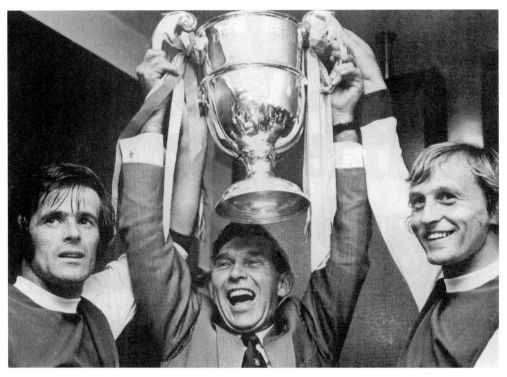

Pat Stanton, Eddie Turnbull and Alan Gordon.

continual interruptions during a team-talk, Turnbull responded by shouting at the politely spoken Gordon: 'the trouble wi' you son is that yir brains are all in yir heid'.

Turnbull liked his players to have their footballing brains firmly tuned in to their feet, and in fairness Gordon was an astute player. With 51 League goals, a League Cup winner's badge, and no fewer than five Hibs hat-tricks to his name, Alan Gordon is a name many Hibernian supporters are familiar with. When you consider that Alan also managed to play with distinction for both Dundee clubs and Hearts too, it is clear he is well known outwith the confines of Easter Road. After all how many players can claim to have played for both Edinburgh and both Dundee clubs?

Born in 1944, Alan started his senior career with Hearts in 1961 and he soon proved himself an efficient goalscorer. He first came to

Hibs' attention in season 1964/65 when he scored twice for Hearts in a 5–3 win at Easter Road. In that season, when Hearts narrowly failed to land the title, he scored 23 times. He went to South Africa in 1967 but was back with Hearts within a year. He joined Dundee United for £8,000 in 1969 and spent three years on Tayside until Eddie Turnbull persuaded him to join Hibs.

It cost Hibs £12,000 to secure his talents but what a bargain that was. He was a Scottish Cup runner-up in 1972 (scoring our goal in the final) and a League Cup winner months later. Alan scored twice in the New Year massacre of Hearts; his second effort struck both posts before crossing the line to make it 7–0.

An elegant striker and an educated man off the field (having studied Economics at Edinburgh University and then switched to Accountancy) he was every bit the cultured footballer. His easy and controlled style was pleasing on the eye and the Edwards, O'Rourke, Gordon, Cropley and Duncan forward-line relied on him more than many appreciated.

His impact was such that many Hibernian supporters are surprised to learn that Alan Gordon was only with Hibs for two years before moving to Dundee. He joined the Dens Park outfit in 1974 for £1,000 more than Hibs had paid and retired in 1976.
Appearances: 84 Goals: 51

GOTTSKALKSSON Olafur

An Icelandic goalkeeper, Olafur unfortunately carried much of the blame when Hibernian were relegated in 1998. Nevertheless he was still with the club when the First Division campaign that followed got underway.

Signed as a twenty-nine-year-old in July 1997, he had 9 Icelandic caps and had been the substitute goalkeeper for his nation no fewer than 30 times. Tall, athletic and a thoroughly nice man he was well liked by the Hibs support but had an alarming tendency to make crucial mistakes at the wrong time.

Prior to playing in Edinburgh he had been with Akranes, FC Rekjavik and Keflavik in Iceland. He moved from Hibernian to Brentford.
Appearances: 63 Goals: 0

GOVAN Jock

Signed from Larkhall Thistle in 1942, Jock Govan was a talented full-back who enjoyed a thirteen-year career at Easter Road. Standing at 5ft 11in and weighing in at just over 12st he was a physically imposing figure.

Born in Larkhall in January 1923, he graduated through the local Academy school into the junior ranks where he was spotted very early by the legendary Hibernian scout Davie Wyper (nicknamed 'Window Wyper'!). Jock remained an apprentice mining engineer and was part-time until he achieved 'time-served' status.

Olafur Gottskalksson, third from left, with Mixu Paatelainen, Justin Skinner, Barry Lavety, Stevie Crawford and Stuart Lovell.

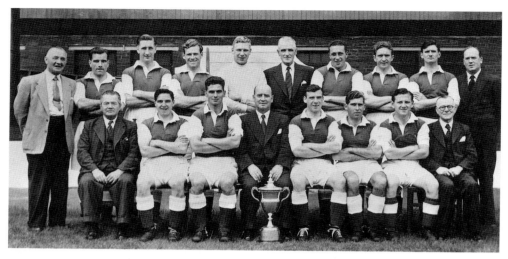

Jock Govan (fourth from right, back row) in Hibernian's Championship-winning team of 1951/52.

Govan formed a solid full-back pairing with Davie Shaw and helped Hibs win the 1948 League Championship – indeed, he missed only one League match in what was Hibs' first post-war trophy success. Later he formed a super partnership with Hugh Howie and both were ever-present when Hibs collected the 1952 title.

Between 1948 and 1949 Jock was capped six times by Scotland. His international career coincided with a period in which Hibs were a major force in the British game. Indeed, when Scotland beat Belgium at Hampden Park in April 1948 there were no fewer than five Hibees in the Scottish team – Shaw, Smith, Combe and Turnbull being the others (in fact Leslie Johnstone of Clyde – an ex-Hibee – played at centre forward).

Jock was noted for his sense of humour and the Hibernian match programme once related the tale of how he and Jimmy Cairns were seen to waltz on the pitch just prior to kick-off in a pre-season friendly in Vienna. It transpired that the match against Rapide was being taken rather seriously by the Austrian football authorities and that the music for the Viennese waltz was intended to take the role

of 'national anthem'. This dawned on Govan and Cairns as they noticed all other twenty players lined up on the halfway line standing stiffly to attention.

In October 1954 Jock left Hibs with Michael Gallacher to join Ayr United and was immediately made the Ayrshire club's captain. The fee for both players was reckoned to be in the region of £3,000 but Jock was freed by United at the end of the 1954/55 season having made a disappointing impression.

After retiring Govan wrote briefly for the *Daily Express* but he soon returned to being a mining engineer before taking early retirement in 1986.

Appearances: 163 Goals: 0

GRAHAM Johnny

Hibs went to Falkirk in November 1969 to sign this rumbustious forward. During his early career he played with Strathclyde Juniors, Third Lanark, and Dundee United.

While at Easter Road, where he was full-time for the first time in his career, his aggressive forward play made him a big favourite. His endeavour was rewarded with a Scottish League cap against England at Coventry. He later moved to Ally MacLeod's Ayr United (in September 1971) and became a great favourite there too before bringing the curtain down on his career with a move back to Falkirk.

Johnny was almost as keen on sailing as he was football and he embarked upon some fairly epic journeys when his career was over. He also ran a successful engineering business, while his son played with and captained Queen's Park.

Appearances: 41 Goals: 14

GRANT Brian

Born in Bannockburn, it was no surprise that Brian made his breakthrough with Stirling Albion. After two years in the lower leagues he moved to Aberdeen. He had a lengthy career there (being awarded a testimonial against Everton) before joining Hibs in the twilight of his career.

Signed in December 1996, he cost in the region of £50,000 and managed a dozen matches in a season that saw Hibs require a play-off victory over Airdrie to retain their Premier League status. He played a clutch of games in Hibernian's relegation season before moving back down the leagues.

Appearances: 17 Goals: 0

GRANT Colin

A centre forward who joined Hibs from Linlithgow Rose in 1965. Two cartilage operations in 1968 severely hampered Colin's progress; between 1965 and 1970 he played just over a dozen League games in a Hibernian jersey.

He became better known after his playing career was over when he fronted the successful Peterhead bid to join the SFL.

Appearances: 14 Goals: 4

GRANT John

John joined Hibs in 1949 from Merchiston Thistle. He settled into full-back duties after

John Grant.

trying various positions and went on to win two caps for Scotland as a defender. In the decade following on from his 1954 debut John made 225 League appearances for Hibs.

In 1964 he joined Raith Rovers but he played for them for only a year before retiring from the game.

Appearances: 225 Goals: 2

GRANT Johnny

Johnny played just a single season for Hibs, and unfortunately for club historians it coincided with the final season of the career of John Grant. But whereas John senior was a defender, young Johnny was a winger. He played 14 League games and scored one goal in the 1963/64 season.

Peter Guggi.

Johnny had been raised in Govan, Glasgow and started his career with the influential Harmony Row Youth Club. From there he moved on to Queen's Park, Ardeer Thistle and Kilwinning Rangers and it was from the latter that Hibernian signed him.

After his short stint at Easter Road he moved to Ayr United in the 1965 close season. Alas, his career at Ayr was short-lived too and he emigrated to South Africa where he played with Durban United.

Appearances: 14 Goals: 1

GRAY Eddie

An inside forward, Gray was signed in 1952 from Kirkintilloch Rob Roy. He was a small player (measuring just 5ft 6in) but was full of energy and desire. Sadly he played only one match in the 1956/57 season.

He spent a brief period on loan to Third Lanark while a Hibee, having been capped by Scotland at school and youth international level.

Appearances: 2 Goals: 1

GUGGI Peter

Signed as a free agent in August 1998, Peter made his debut against Hamilton Accies in a League Cup tie. He showed neat touches and was soon popping in the odd goal, Ayr United being early victims. However, he fell out of favour not long after arriving and left rather quietly within a matter of months.

Peter had played with Rapid Vienna and is an Austrian national.

Appearances: 8 Goals: 2

GUNN Bryan

Signed from Norwich City by Alex McLeish, Bryan Gunn's signing typified Hibs' desperate bid to stay in the Premier League. He was a vastly experienced 'keeper having played several times for Scotland and been a regular at Norwich City.

Alas, for all Gunn's undoubted experience, he was unable to keep Hibs in the top flight. Worse was to follow when he was injured in a freak training ground accident and his career was virtually over thereafter. He returned to East Anglia to take up a goal-keepers' coaching course.

He had been born in Thurso in 1963 and had been an understudy to Jim Leighton at Aberdeen until moving to Norwich City for £100,000 in 1986.

Appearances: 12 Goals: 0

GUNNING James

A single outing in the 1950/51 season was the total extent of James' career as a Hibee. Raised in Helensburgh, he joined Wolverhampton Wanderers as a youngster but was unable to settle and moved to Hibs in 1946 as an amateur. He joined the RAF and a Highland posting enabled him to play with Forres Mechanics.

When his RAF service ended he returned to Easter Road but found openings extremely limited. A tricky outside right he moved to Manchester City in November 1950 and he made 13 outings for the Maine Road club before bringing the curtain down on his senior career with Barrow.

Appearances: 1 Goals: 0

H

HALL Alec

Alas, an entry in the one-game wonders column for Mr Hall. His only outing in earnest came in the 1946/47 season. He had served Hibs during the war period but was essentially only with Hibernian on loan from Sunderland. Prior to playing in the northeast of England he had been with Dunfermline.

Appearances: 1 Goals: 0

HAMILL Hugh

Joined the club in the early 1980s, but saw his career badly hampered by a leg break. Born in Dumbarton he was a wing-half in the old-fashioned mould. He played 7 League games while a Hibee.

Appearances: 7 Goals: 0

HAMILTON Brian

A talented left-sided midfielder, Brian impressed with St Mirren, helping them to the Scottish Cup in 1987. His signing by Hibs in July 1989 was viewed as something of a coup and his silky skills were soon put to good use.

Capped four times by Scotland at Under-21 level he was a very popular Hibee and regarded as a player's player due to his tremendous workrate. A League Cup winner in 1991 he seldom missed games as his fitness was excellent and his temperament equally reliable. There was consternation on the

Brian Hamilton.

Easter Road terraces therefore when Brian 'jumped ship' in January 1995 to join fierce rivals Hearts.

He was predictably a success at Tynecastle and later served Falkirk and Clydebank.

Appearances: 194 Goals: 10

HAMILTON Donald

Yet another in the list of young goalkeepers who flitted in and out of Easter Road in the 1950s. Donald made 17 outings in the 1953/54 season and 5 in the next term. Signed from Armadale Thistle in 1953, he was quite small for a goalkeeper and did not last beyond the two seasons as a Hibee.

Appearances: 23 Goals: 0

HAMILTON Johnny

Signed as an eighteen-year-old from Cumbernauld Juniors by Bob Shankly. A clever midfielder, his left footed skills were delightful and it was always going to be a difficult task to hold on to such a natural talent. Between 1969 and 1973 Johnny made 58 League appearances for Hibs.

In due course this rather stocky player moved on to Rangers. He enjoyed some success at Ibrox but did not wholly fit in with Jock Wallace's work ethic. He later played with Millwall and St Johnstone.

Appearances: 58 Goals: 11

HAMILTON Willie

One of the most enigmatic performers ever to pull on a Hibs jersey, Hamilton could be sublime – a near genius – but like so many genius footballers he was essentially a flawed character. A lack of dedication and a fondness for the good life were ultimately his undoing.

There were games where he dominated the scene magnificently, arguably never more so than in a friendly against the mighty Real Madrid at Easter Road as he inspired Hibs to a 2–0 win.

Willie Hamilton.

William Murdoch Hamilton began his senior career at Sheffield United in 1956. In 1961 he made a £12,000 move north to Middlesbrough but he was not a hit on Teeside and in June 1962 Hearts were able to secure his services for a mere £5,000.

He was nothing short of sensational for Hearts and won a League Cup winner's medal in 1962. However, he fell out of favour and the excellent *Hearts in Art* by Andrew Hoggan suggests that 'his career went off the rails during the long winter shut down of 1962/63'.

In October 1963 Hibernian shelled out £6,000 and he quickly regained all his old magic. As well as the Real Madrid match there were regular highlights and Willie proved a hero to a whole generation of Hibs fans who were prepared to forgive his poor workrate because it was more than compensated for by sheer natural talent. When Hibs bundled Rangers out of the 1965 Scottish Cup competition it was on the back of a two-goal salvo by Hamilton in a 2–1 win.

It was not just Hibernian fans who loved Willie. Those in charge of Scotland's affairs were impressed too and he gained his only Scotland cap while a Hibee. Thus he had much gratitude to the then Hibs boss, Jock Stein, as it was Stein who instilled an unlikely level of self-belief in the enigmatic inside forward.

He helped Hibs win the Summer Cup in 1964, scoring in the replayed final against Aberdeen when Hibs won 3–1. However, his off field activities and lack of dedication to mundane aspects of football – like training – eventually convinced Hibs to off-load him. The fact that Aston Villa were prepared to pay £25,000 for him in August 1965 was some consolation.

His spell with Aston Villa was wrecked by a car crash and although he recovered, returned to Hearts and even played abroad, his career was in decline. He was in South Africa in 1969, with Ross County in 1970 and Hamilton Accies in 1971.

Sadly Willie died young. He was not yet forty when he passed away in 1976 and was mourned on both sides of Edinburgh such was his popularity.
Appearances: 50 Goals: 15

HARPER Joe

A small, barrel-chested striker, Joseph Montgomery Harper was one of the finest goal-grabbers of his era. He started his career with Morton in the mid-1960s and then, following a glut of goals, moved to Huddersfield Town. Failing to settle in West Yorkshire, he returned to Morton and in March 1969 he scored a hat-trick for the Greenock club against Hibernian at Cappielow.

Joe Harper.

From Morton his travels took him northwards to Aberdeen then south to Everton. His boss at Aberdeen had been Eddie Turnbull and when Eddie became Hibs' manager he was swift to lure Harper to Edinburgh.

It cost Hibernian a club record £120,000 to secure his services (indeed, that was the Scottish record fee at the time) but he was a proven goalscorer and he did not let anyone in Edinburgh down.

Joe had many highs in his Hibernian career, short as it was. He scored our first ever Premier League goal when we beat Hearts 1–0 and scored all five in a 5–0 win over Nijmegan (he also hit the post in that game!). I once asked Joe which was his favourite Hibernian memory and he did not hesitate to answer: 'The 1975 League Cup final, or as it's better known the 6–3 game when myself and Dixie Deans of Celtic both scored hat-tricks. After the game people asked me how I felt about scoring a hat-trick and still losing. My answer was, "Okay we haven't won the cup but I had a job to do as a striker. When you go out in a cup final and

score a hat-trick you have to be pleased." I had done my bit and scored three times against the biggest club in the land.'

As football historian Bob Crampsey remarked 'no man ever played better in a losing cause'.

He left Hibs in 1976 to rejoin Aberdeen for the ludicrously low sum of £40,000 and went on to become a Dons legend. From 1976 to 1981 he was their main marksman and he scored 57 goals in only 105 League appearances for the Dons.

After his senior playing career ended he played briefly in the Highland League with Peterhead then managed both Huntly and Deveronvale before returning to the West of Scotland and renewing his association with Morton as part of their commercial team.
Appearances: 69 Goals: 26

HARPER Kevin

Born in Oldham in January 1976, this clever little winger joined Hibs in 1992 as an apprentice and was promptly capped at Youth, Under-21 and 'B' international level. Tricky, direct and useful around goal he became a Hibs favourite very quickly.

It was an Under-21 hat-trick that finally propelled Kevin Harper from local to national stage. His 1995 threesome against Finland – one with his right, one with his left and a header – neatly proved his versatility.

When Hibs slipped into the First Division it was clear he would be looking to move on and in September 1998 he joined Derby County. Later in his career he served Portsmouth.
Appearances: 96 Goals: 15

HARRIS Colin

Between 1984 and 1986, Colin made 26 outings in a Hibs jersey, one of which was in the 1986 League Cup final against Aberdeen.

The highlight of his time at Easter Road may very well have been his first goal for the club, which came late in a 2–1 win over Rangers. However, in a nutshell he was not one of John Blackley's most successful signings and he was allowed to leave Hibs by Alex Miller for Raith Rovers in 1986.

His was to prove a slightly nomadic career path – Raith Rovers, Dundee, Hibernian, Raith Rovers, Hamilton, Meadowbank, Clydebank and Queen of the South. He was most successful at Hamilton where he scored a winner in the B&Q Cup final, picked up another winner's badge twelve months later and won a First Division Championship badge.

Colin could play in goal and did so on more than one occasion for Accies.

Appearances: 26 Goals: 4

HARROWER Jim

Born in Alva in August 1935, Jim was a prolific marksman in junior football with Sauchie, Kilsyth Rangers and Bo'ness United. It was from the lattermost of these that Hibs signed him and he broke into the Hibs first team in season 1955/56. He showed enough promise to tempt Liverpool to sign him in January 1958. In all he scored 11 goals in 36 Hibs League matches.

He was with Liverpool from 1957 to 1960 and scored 21 goals in 96 League matches. From Liverpool he moved to Newcastle United, where he played just five games, then Falkirk. He later played with St Johnstone and at one stage in his Perth career threatened legal action against the SFA when handed a 28-day suspension.

Capped once by Scotland at Under-23 level he was the archetypal inside forward – a raider who could both create and take chances.

Appearances: 36 Goals: 11

HARTLEY Paul

Signed by Alex McLeish from Raith Rovers for £200,000, Paul helped in the push to promo-

Paul Hartley.

tion from the First Division in 1999. However, he never quite made the same impression when Hibs played in the Premier League and he was allowed to join St Johnstone.

He had in fact been a Hibernian 'S' form but joined Hamilton on a YTS programme and made his debut for Accies when only seventeen. He spent three years with Hamilton, but never once played at Douglas Park, as the Lanarkshire club sought a new ground.

Jimmy Nicholl bought him for Millwall (one of four Scots signed on the same day!) but Paul did not settle in London and followed Nicholl back to Scotland with Raith Rovers.

By 2003 his skills were back on show in the top flight, albeit with Hearts! And in the New Year clash of 2005 he scored the Hearts equaliser in a derby 1–1 draw.

Appearances: 26 Goals: 6

HARVEY Graham

Born in Musselburgh in 1961, Graham moved from Ormiston Primrose to Dundee in 1985. A 5ft 11in striker he was a steady if unspectacular marksman for the 'Dee.

From 1982 to 1985 he was in and out of the Hibernian side and his return of 3 goals in 31 matches was probably a little less than was expected.

Appearances: 31 Goals: 3

HAZEL John

Often the twelfth man in the team known as Turnbull's Tornadoes, he made his first-team debut against Hearts at Tynecastle in an East of Scotland Shield game in May 1970. At the same venue he scored a vital Scottish Cup goal in 1971.

John had had a choice of clubs and one-time Hearts boss Bobby Seith nearly took him to Preston North End. There is no doubt he was a talented youngster, as his four Scotland Youth caps prove.

In and out of the side, his misfortune was to try and earn a place in the Edwards, O'Rourke, Gordon, Cropley and Duncan forward-line. It was only when he moved on to Morton that he earned regular first-team football.

Appearances: 43 Goals: 3

HENDRY Ian

A tragic debutant, Ian suffered a compound fracture just twenty seconds into his inaugural match at Berwick in January 1980. Signed as a twenty-one-year-old from Cambridge United, he would make only two appearances for Hibs in his short career.

Appearances: 2 Goals: 0

HENRY Fabrice

A French midfielder, his career began in 1982 with Sochaux. He stayed there for eleven years and gained French Under-21 recognition. He joined Marseille for one year before moving to Toulouse and then, in June 1986, moved to Spain with Toledo, before sampling Switzerland with Basle.

Born in Paris in 1968, he joined Hibs in the summer of 1999 and made his debut in the opening League fixture against Motherwell. Thereafter he was used rather sparingly before being released, having failed to fulfil the expectations placed on his experienced shoulders.

Appearances: 9 Goals: 0

HERRIOT Jim

Born in Airdrie in 1939, Jim joined Dunfermline from Douglasdale Juniors in 1958. He was a capable 'keeper, played in the 1965 Scottish Cup final, and went on to win eight Scotland caps and several Under-23 awards.

Sold by Dunfermline to Birmingham City in May 1965, he played in 200 matches for the Brummies before moving to Mansfield Town.

He joined Hibs in 1971 from Durban City after Hibernian had endured a nightmare tour of the north of England in which young 'keeper Eddie Pryde had struggled to prove that he was ready for league action.

Jim won a League Cup final medal and a Dryburgh Cup badge while with Hibs. He was also the last line of defence in the 1972 Scottish Cup final which Hibs lost 6–1 to Celtic.

His name lives on in literary circles, having been 'used' by the author of the famous veterinary books set in the Yorkshire Dales. Many Scottish football fans remember him as the goalkeeper who blackened out the skin under his eyes to counter any glare.

Appearances: 57 Goals: 0

HIGGINS Tony

Never the most elegant footballer, Tony was a big bustling midfielder, who could also play up front. He joined Hibs in July 1972. His debut came soon afterwards in a League Cup tie against Aberdeen and he became one of Eddie Turnbull's favourite players.

Eddie Turnbull knew that Tony was keen to complete his higher education and therefore suggested that Tony was initially part-time, but so taken was he by life as a professional footballer, Tony soon went full-time and put his education 'on ice'. His career at Hibs went well and he scored a rather useful 23 goals in 104 League fixtures.

In March 1980 Higgins moved to Partick Thistle but he later formed a formidable (and sizable!) partnership with Andy Ritchie at Morton.

Appearances: 104 Goals: 23

HIGGINS Hugh

A useful junior with Bonnybridge and Tranent, Hibs had to beat off competition from Celtic and Sunderland to secure this young forward.

His debut came in a 3–3 draw with Spurs in 1956; replacing the injured Gordon Smith he stunned all and sundry by scoring the final Hibs goal.

Alas, such a promising start was not to signal a lengthy career in green and white. Hugh went to Third Lanark on loan in December 1957 before making a permanent move to Dunfermline in November 1958. He actually played only 10 matches as a Hibee.

Appearances: 10 Goals: 0

HIGGINS John

Between 1954 and 1956 this dark-haired full-back made a dozen outings as a Hibee. However, he was unable to forge a lengthy career at Easter Road. Thereafter he served St Mirren, Swindon and Ayr United.

Appearances: 12 Goals: 0

HIGGINS Laurie

A winger, Laurie was signed from Edinburgh Thistle and lived in Musselburgh. He played a single game in the 1950/51 campaign and eventually joined Aberdeen in 1953.

Appearances: 1 Goals: 0

HILLAND Paul

A product of the Hibernian youth system, young Paul was not quite able to convince Bobby Williamson that he was the defender of his dreams. There were three League outings at the end of season 2001/02 and a brief loan spell at Cowdenbeath but ultimately no more than that with Hibs.

Appearances: 3 Goals: 0

HENDERSON Martin

In early 1978 Hibs went to Rangers to secure the services of gangly striker Martin Henderson. A straightforward, no frills centre forward, Henderson had bagged his share of goals at Rangers but in truth never looked likely to create his own quota at Hibs.

His spell as a Hibee was a three-month loan arrangement and he later played in the United States and with Leicester City in England.

Appearances: 6 Goals: 0

HOGG Davie

Joined Hibs as a seventeen-year-old in 1963 and had the distinction of being Jock Stein's first Hibs signing. Unfortunately he quickly gave up full-time football in order to work full time in insurance. It was hardly surprising as he had shown an academic bent at Holy Cross Academy, which led to him being offered a chance to study languages at Edinburgh University.

Given a free transfer in 1968 he moved to Dundee United then Hamilton and Alloa. Hogg netted a solitary goal in his 10 matches at Easter Road.

Appearances: 10 Goals: 1

HOLSGROVE Paul

During Alex McLeish's reign a number of players enjoyed brief cameo appearances for Hibs. Paul Holsgrove was one such player.

Signed on the eve of the 1998/99 First Division campaign he ghosted in and out of the Hibernian midfield without ever imposing himself fully. Perhaps Paul can be accurately described as a 'journeyman' player having played with the likes of Aldershot, Luton, Millwall and Reading before coming to Hibernian.

Appearances: 17 Goals: 1

HOUCHEN Keith

Keith's senior career began in 1977 and he quickly served a number of clubs, including Hartlepool, Orient, York City, Scunthorpe and Coventry City. It was while with the latter that he gained national prominence by scoring with a diving header in the 1987 FA Cup final against Tottenham Hotspur which Coventry won 3–2.

He joined Hibs in March 1988 and operated largely as a target man. There is no doubt he made the perfect start with a goal against Hearts within twenty-five minutes of his debut.

However the gloss soon began to wear off and he fell into the fans' bad-books when he gestured towards them following sustained barracking in a Skol Cup tie against Raith Rovers. That incident was reported to the SFA and when he was sent off late on during a victory over St Johnstone his frustration was clear for all to see.

Despite that debut goal at Tynecastle and a vital winner against Rangers at Ibrox in March 1990 his career fizzled out at Hibs and he was soon on his way back to England.

Appearances: 57 Goals: 11

HOWIE Hugh

The cold statistics show that Hugh Howie played in 139 League matches without scoring a single goal. It is therefore a surprise to

Hugh Howie.

learn that Hugh is remembered for not one, but two goals that he scored in his career. One was a legendary Scottish Cup semi-final winner the other was an international debut goal!

Hugh was something of a utility player and far more skilful than many observers realised. He started his football with Hallside Juveniles then moved on to Newton Juniors and it was from there that Hibs signed him in 1943. Despite having a career that was disrupted by illness and injury there is no doubt Hugh made a significant impact as a Hibee.

A tall man (he measured just under the 6ft mark) he was a lithe 11st 12lbs and could move with surprising speed. Very capable at left-back, Hugh could also play as a centre half and, while not a noted goalscorer, he did score one famous counter in a Scottish Cup semi-final against Motherwell. That goal has become one of the most talked about goals in Hibernian's rich history.

The 1946/47 season attracted huge crowds as the game returned to normality after the war years. Hibernian battled through to the semi-final stage of the national cup only to come up against a resolute Motherwell. In the era before penalty shoot-outs, it was decided to play the game to a finish. It was 1–1 after 90 minutes had elapsed and thus the game went into a 'golden goal' period which would not end until one side scored. Ultimately the match lasted an astonishing 142 minutes until Howie scored in spectacular fashion. A long punt upfield by the Motherwell goalkeeper Johnston was returned back over his head and into the net.

Ever present in the 1951/52 title-winning side, Hugh played a peripheral role in the other two championship-winning sides.

Hugh was capped once by Scotland, against Wales in the 1948/49 season, and he made it a memorable occasion by scoring a goal. Remarkably, although Howie did not feature in the next Scotland game Hibs still supplied both full-backs. It was a measure of the strength in depth that Hibs had that Jock Govan neatly slipped in to partner Davie Shaw.

After retiring Hugh took up journalism and he was occupied in that capacity until he lost his life in a motor accident in January 1958.
Appearances: 139 Goals: 0

HUGGINS Dave

Born in Edinburgh in 1962, Dave joined Hibernian straight from Tynecastle Boys Club. He made his goalkeeping debut against Morton in April 1980 and, as a Scottish schoolboy cap, was expected to show up well.

He made three appearances in season 1979/80, but it was not a good season to make your Hibs bow as the club slid into the First Division, despite the presence (at times!) of George Best.
Appearances: 3 Goals: 0

HUGHES John

John Hughes was actually aged twenty-three when he finally made it into the ranks of professional football, joining Berwick after an abortive spell with Arbroath and having reverted to junior football with Newtongrange Star.

From Berwick, Hughes, who was nicknamed 'Yogi', moved to Wales with Swansea. Jim Jefferies signed Hughes for Falkirk and the big centre half never looked back. He won two First Division championships with the Bairns and was a 'man-mountain' of a captain.

He switched to Celtic in a £250,000 deal. A Leith-bred player, John was happy at Celtic but maintained that he was delighted when Hibernian stepped in to sign him in October 1996. Quickly made club captain he was the type of hero figure with whom the Hibernian support was able to establish a huge rapport.

John Hughes.

Mind you he had a torrid introduction to life as a Hibee. In his first game Hibs were crushed 2–4 at Kilmarnock and his second game was worse. He was sent off against Hearts in the derby at Tynecastle.

John helped Hibs battle out of the First Division but as time crept on he was allowed to leave and join Ayr United. Ironically, he was in the Ayr side that dumped Hibs from the League Cup in the 2002 semi-final.
Appearances: 71 Goals: 4

HUGHES Pat

Pat was a tall left-sided player who joined the club in 1955 from Whitburn Juniors. Despite never being one of the star names at Easter Road he did accumulate a respectable 68 League matches in his eight years at the club. Forfar Athletic used his services in the 1964/65 campaign but twenty-five matches later he hung up his boots.
Appearances: 68 Goals: 0

HUNTER Willie

Joined Hibernian in 1969 following a spell in America with Detroit Cougars, but it was as one of Motherwell's Ancell Babes that he had made his name.

How unfortunate that Willie did not join Hibernian as a youth – for he was a keen Hibs fan and a native of Edinburgh's Abbeyhill district. Nevertheless he made light of his late arrival and gave some inspired performances in 1969. His debut came in February against Clyde and he nabbed his first goal for the club against Morton. In truth his role was helping to bring on the younger players around him but perhaps Willie had missed his chance for he soon drifted from the picture.

He travelled to South Africa to end his playing career and then was assistant manager at Portsmouth to his former 'Well teammate Ian St John. He later managed Queen of the South and Inverness Thistle in his own right.
Appearances: 11 Goals: 1

HUNTER Gordon

Gordon had a strange start to his Hibs career. Bertie Auld signed him in 1983 only to be sacked twenty-four hours later! Fortunately the subsequent manager Pat Stanton kept Hunter on and thirteen years of loyal service followed. A wonderfully perceptive centre half he was also noted for his fairness in his desire to win.

Picking highlights from such a lengthy career is never easy but a few do stand out. In August 1994 Gordon entered Hibernian history when he ended the nightmare run of 22 consecutive games against Hearts without victory. He scored the only goal of a derby match at Tynecastle in the sixty-second minute of the game at the Gorgie Road end and the press photograph of Gordon leaping into the crowd to celebrate was an enduring image.

To this day Gordon has mixed feelings about that goal: '… it was embarrassing that it took so long to end that miserable run and if someone else could have scored a derby winner in half the time I would have been happier'.

Gordon, who was not the tallest of centre-backs, was the lynchpin in Alex Miller's defence and won a League Cup winner's medal in 1991 against Dunfermline Athletic. Hibs, having beaten Rangers 1–0 at Hampden in an epic semi-final, had understandably high hopes for the final but it was not a foregone conclusion and Gordon played with his customary concentration to ensure the trophy came back to Easter Road.

It was doubly satisfying for Gordon as he had been an eighteen-year-old in the Hibernian side beaten by Aberdeen in the 1985 League Cup final. Remarkably he played in three finals, the last one being the

Gordon Hunter.

1993 match against Rangers at Celtic Park that Hibs lost 1–2.

He was granted a testimonial in September 1996 and Coventry City provided the opposition. He was sent off twice in his Hibernian career; coincidentally on both occasions while in direct opposition to Mark Hateley of Rangers.

Appearances: 339 Goals: 8

HURTADO Eduardo

An Ecuadorian centre forward, it appeared that Eduardo (or 'The Tank' as he was nicknamed) was past his best when he joined Hibs. Alex McLeish signed him as Hibs had made a faltering start to the 2001/02 season, but sadly the big centre was unable to reverse things.

He stood at 6ft 3in and weighed over 14st but the important statistic was that he had scored 43 goals in 71 international outings for Ecuador. Ulises De La Cruz, the Hibs full-back, was a welcoming teammate for Eduardo.

Hurtado was seen as a direct replacement for Mixu Paatelainen, who had moved to Strasbourg, and Craig Brewster who was out injured. Having played with Colo Colo (Chile), Los Angeles Galaxy and New England Revolution in America and Liga Deportivo Universitario of Quito in Ecuador as well as St Gallen in Switzerland much was expected of him.

Ultimately Hurtado proved slow and cumbersome and other than goals against St Johnstone and Stranraer (in the cup) did little to impress. He was released when Bobby Williamson took over from Franck Sauzee.

Appearances: 12 Goals: 1

HUTCHINSON Bobby

Signed in November 1977 from Dundee in the deal that took Erich Schaedler to Dens Park, Bobby was a forward with an eye for goal and made his Hibs debut against Partick Thistle at Easter Road in November 1977.

Bobby had a bit of a purple patch in late 1978, scoring in three consecutive League games and overall he bagged 13 goals in 68 League matches.

Born in Glasgow's Gorbals district in 1954, his previous clubs had included Queens Park juniors, Aberdeen Lads Club, Montrose and Dundee.

Appearances: 68 Goals: 13

I

IRVINE Willie (1)

Started his career with Stirling Albion in 1982, joining them from Dunipace Juniors. He was a powerful forward for them and scored five times in the famous 20–0 Scottish Cup demolition of Selkirk in 1984. Indeed, he scored 25 goals that season and 20 the next – which was sufficient to lure Hibs to buy him for £35,000 in June 1986.

His career at Easter Road saw him make a quite stunning start. He had a goal in a friendly against Seville and then two days later bagged a hat-trick against Chelsea. But such a prolific rate proved impossible to maintain and he scored twice in six games over the remainder of the season, both goals coming in a 3–2 win over Clydebank. It was however at a time when Hibs were not scoring enough goals generally and Willie was not to stay long.

From Easter Road Willie's career carried him to Dunfermline, FR Vidar (Norway), Airdrie, Meadowbank and Berwick Rangers before he settled with Alloa Athletic. He proved himself a prolific marksman for the Wasps but it was his unwilling part in a siege at Glenochil Prison that catapulted his name into the national newspapers. He emerged unscathed from that incident and continued to give Alloa excellent service into the early 2000s.

Appearances: 12 Goals: 2

IRVINE Willie (2)

Best known for the striking partnership he forged with Steve Cowan, Irvine was a quick striker whose approach to the game was fairly direct.

Willie began his senior career with Celtic, signing for Jock Stein's club in 1973 as a sixteen-year-old. Competition was inevitably keen at Parkhead and he was freed in 1977 having failed to reach the first team.

He then went from junior football to Alloa Athletic, bagged 29 goals in a season and in 1979 Motherwell snapped him up for £25,000. In the Steelmen's promotion winning team of 1981/82 he was top scorer with 21 goals. However, like manager Davie Hay, he was to leave in the shadow of that triumph, electing to move to Hibernian.

While at Hibs he was the second-top scorer in the Premier League during the 1983/84 campaign. Such was his prowess that it was suggested the club rejected a £150,000 offer from Aberdeen for Irvine's services.

Willie was nicknamed 'Noddy' by virtue of his unusual running style and if he had a fault it was perhaps that he was exceedingly left-sided. He spent a period on loan to Falkirk at the tail end of the 1985/86 season before joining Ayr United.

Appearances: 100 Goals: 29

J

JACK Mathias

A powerful German-born defender who could also occupy the holding midfield berth, Mathias joined Hibernian in July 1999 and provided much needed muscle to a

Mathias Jack (right) fends off Kemble of St Johnstone.

Hibernian side that was increasingly earning respect for its flair. He was a rather combative player whose name found its way into referee's notebooks with alarming frequency.

He was a vastly experienced performer, having played in Germany with Stahl Brandenburg, VFL Odenburgh, Rot Weiss Essen, Bochum and Fortuna Dusseldorf.

He was out of contract at Easter Road in the summer of 2002 and spent a brief time looking for a club before Bobby Williamson offered him a single year 'extension'. However, he played very few games in the 2002/03 season.

Mathias was enigmatic in that his growling persona on the pitch was offset by a lovely friendly manner off the field that made him a pleasure to chat to.

Appearances: 90 Goals: 4

JACKSON Chris

Signed in May 1991 from Salveson BC. He scored early in his career against Hearts at Tynecastle and this, along with his distinctive ginger hair, ensured he stood out.

He was never quite able to grab an automatic spot and eventually moved on to Stirling Albion. Chris then had the pleasure of coming back to haunt Hibs, scoring the winner in a replay, as Albion knocked us out of the Scottish Cup in season 1998/99. From Stirling Albion he moved on to Stenhousemuir.

Appearances: 70 Goals: 2

JACKSON Darren

One of the more extrovert players in recent times, Jackson had a natural ability that encompassed not just playing but upsetting referees and opposition supporters. Yet when he concentrated on the game he was a wonderfully talented player capable of moments of sublime ability.

Darren Jackson.

A proven goalscorer, he initially served Meadowbank Thistle, Newcastle United and Dundee United – where he rarely failed to excite. He played for Dundee United in the epic 1991 Scottish Cup final against Motherwell (which United lost 3–4 despite a Jackson goal).

When moving from Newcastle to Dundee United he cost £200,000 and this was indication of the latent talent that lurked beneath a rather spiky exterior.

Darren joined Hibernian in the summer of 1992 and scored 13 goals in his first League season as a Hibee. Indeed, he remained a frequent marksman for Hibs over the next five seasons and must have caused consternation when he scored the winner for Hibs in the 1993 League Cup semi-final against his former Dundee United employees. He scored 50 goals in 172 League matches and was rarely missing from first-team action due to his super fitness.

Darren spent more time with Hibernian than at any of his eight other senior clubs, which is a measure in itself of how much he enjoyed Easter Road.

He moved to Celtic in the close season of 1997 for £1.5 million, which was a good return for Hibernian, but his time at Parkhead was blighted by a serious illness that required a brain operation to rectify. Later Darren played for Hearts, Livingston, St Johnstone and Clydebank and he was a noted Scotland international.

Appearances: 172 Goals: 50

JAMES Craig

Signed by Bobby Williamson on loan from Sunderland in 2002, Craig was a left wing-back and spent the bulk of the 2002/03 season at Easter Road. He performed well and scored a few goals, including one in the amazing 4–4 derby draw at Tynecastle.

Sadly Hibs could not offer him a full-time contract and he returned to Sunderland for the 2003/04 season when the Black Cats found themselves in Division One.

Appearances: 22 Goals: 2

JAMIESON Willie

A tall and powerful youngster, Willie broke into the Hibs side in the early 1980s and provided a glut of goals. The fact that he was comfortable at either centre half or centre forward enhanced his prospects no end.

He won a First Division Championship badge at Easter Road in 1981 but was rather surprisingly allowed to leave on a free transfer some four years later. His Easter Road career had run from 1980 to 1985 and brought 27 goals from 117 League matches.

John Lambie signed him for Hamilton and what an astute move that proved; Willie helped Accies to two First Division titles. He joined Dundee in 1990 and won a Centenary Cup medal at Fir Park in 1990 before adding another First Division badge two years later.

His career thereafter carried him to Partick Thistle, Hearts and Ayr United. He was with the Honest Men when they landed the 1997

Willie Jamieson.

Second Division Championship and in the summer of 1998 joined Partick Thistle as assistant manager.

Appearances: 117 Goals: 27

JEAN Earl

Signed in the 1999/2000 season, Earl made just five outings as a substitute and failed to make the impression hoped for.

He was born in St Lucia in 1971 and joined Hibs with a solid reputation having picked up 68 international caps and served clubs in Portugal (Olieveirense, Lecca and Selgoireas) and England (Ipswich, Rotherham and Plymouth). A trial period when Hibs were in the Caribbean during the winter shutdown convinced Alex McLeish that the man from the bizarrely named club, Joe Public, could prove useful.

Unfortunately he never really adapted to the rigours of the Scottish game and was released in the summer of 2000.

Appearances: 5 Goals: 0

JOHNSTONE Leslie

Joined Hibs in February 1947 from Clyde and made a fairly spectacular start, netting four goals in the 7–1 demolition of Airdrie. However, he could not gain a permanent berth in the side, which led to him leaving with the remarkable statistics of having played 9 games and scored 8 goals!

He moved back to Clyde in October 1947 having cost Hibs £10,000 to lure eastwards. That £10,000 fee was, at the time, a Scottish record fee, being the first ever five-figure deal.

Appearances: 9 Goals: 8

JOHNSTONE Bobby

Nicknamed 'Nicker' by dint of his scurrying, probing, football he was in some ways the classic small Scottish inside forward. His forte was not speed, nor was it strength, rather it was an ability to dart between opponents, pass with unerring accuracy and entertain with his natural ball skills. That he was also a considerable goalscorer made him the complete footballer in his era. That much was recognised when Manchester City paid the then sizable sum of £22,000 to prise him away from Edinburgh in 1955.

Born and bred in the lovely border town of Selkirk, he joined Willie McCartney's Hibernian in 1946. He was only seventeen at the time. The diminutive apprentice painter made traditional progress through the Hibernian reserve team before breaking into the first team in the late 1940s. His name was to be the final piece in the 'Famous Five' jigsaw and for almost a decade Easter Road became synonymous with great entertaining football.

A simple glance at the record books will reveal just how good a player Bobby was. He won 17 caps for Scotland (scoring half a dozen goals), won two League Championship badges with Hibs (1951 and 1952) and scored in two consecutive FA Cup finals (lifting the cup in the second of those finals).

But such statistics, however impressive, tell only part of the story. Ian Wood, veteran journalist of *The Scotsman*, illustrated this superbly when he recalled that legendary cricket commentator John Arlott had once said he: '… took five great memories of Edinburgh back to England – Smith, Johnstone, Reilly, Turnbull and Ormond'.

Bobby Johnstone represented Great Britain in 1955 when the combined home nations tackled the Rest of Europe in what was a tremendous accolade for any player. Bobby responded to the big stage in typical fashion – by scoring.

Bobby enjoyed two spells with Hibernian. As mentioned above he moved to Manchester City in 1955 but in 1959 he returned to Easter Road and stayed long enough to rack up his 100th League goal for the club. His travels would take him back to Lancashire (this time with Oldham) and he stayed in the north west of England well beyond his footballing years before returning to Selkirk.

By having played in the 'Famous Five' Bobby's place in Hibernian history is firmly cemented. By having exposed his talents to wider audiences in England, and beyond, his reputation as a very clever footballer is equally assured.

Appearances: 195 Goals: 100

JONES Mervyn

Between 1969 and 1971 left-back Mervyn Jones played 30 League games for Hibs. His was one of those short Hibernian careers that covered just a couple of seasons and promised far more than it ultimately delivered.

After leaving Hibs Mervyn served Falkirk, Stirling Albion and Cowdenbeath.

Appearances: 30 Goals: 0

Bobby Johnstone.

K

KANE John

A youngster who made his debut as a substitute against Livingston in April 2004. Touted as a utility player who could play both defence and midfield, he stood out from the crowd by dint of his shock of vivid blond hair. Born in Glasgow in 1987, he was a product of the club's youth system

Appearances: 1 Goals: 0

KANE Paul

Paul's father, Jimmy Kane, was on Hibs' books briefly before moving to Cowdenbeath in November 1959 without ever having played a League match. Paul on the other hand made over 200 outings as a Hibee and became one of the most popular Hibs players of the modern era.

Kane joined Hibs in 1982 and, as a life-long fan brought up in Leith, was delighted to do so. His game contained plenty of energy and sufficient strength to make him as combative a midfielder as any in the game at one stage.

By 1986 he was part of the Hibs side that lost the League Cup final to Aberdeen 0–3; indeed, Aberdeen knocked Hibs out of the Scottish Cup at the semi-final stage and Kane in later years would say that facing the experienced Alex McLeish, Willie Miller and Jim Leighton came just too soon for a young Hibs team.

October 1987 gave the Hibs-daft Paul one of his finest memories. He scored the winning goal at Easter Road as Hibernian defeated Hearts 2–1 and – in an era in which Hearts largely held the upper hand – it was clearly a special moment.

Kane spent nine seasons at Easter Road before moving on to Oldham and indeed was barely out of the door when the Wallace Mercer takeover bid surfaced. It says much

Paul Kane.

for Paul's Hibernian leanings that he travelled up from Oldham to help in the 'Hands Off Hibs' movement.

From Oldham he journeyed to Alex Smith's Aberdeen in November 1991 but he left Pittodrie to join Viking Stavanger of Norway in Scotland's first ever Bosman transfer.

He came back to Scotland when he was thirty-one and played with St Johnstone then Clyde before retiring in the summer of 2003 having completed twenty years in the senior game.

Appearances: 247 Goals: 33

KEAN Sammy

Wing-half Sammy Kean played a key role in the Hibernian team which won the Scottish League Championship in 1948. A native of Dumbarton, he made a major contribution to the success enjoyed in the post-war era, although his work was often overshadowed by that of the more illustrious forward line – the 'Famous Five'.

Signed from Kirkintilloch Rob Roy in 1938 by Willie McCartney, he went on to win international honours with the Scottish League but the war badly disrupted his career.

In 1941, he teamed up with war-time guest player Matt Busby to form one of the strongest half-back lines in Scotland, and Kean always believed the pair's best performance together was the game when Hibs fought back from 0–2 down to take the Summer Cup from Rangers in 1941. Among the interesting items the winning Hibs players received was a specially commissioned recording of the BBC Radio commentary.

Such was Kean's prowess, he and Tommy McIntyre were the subject of a £10,000 bid from Manchester United before the war… which Hibs turned down.

Never the most prolific of marksmen, he did however grab a goal in the Scottish Cup thriller against Raith Rovers that Hibs won 4–3 at Kirkcaldy in 1949, and he had been a scorer from all of 60 yards when Lawrie Reilly made his Hibs debut. A far less happy cup memory was being part of the Hibernian side sensationally ditched from the competition by little Edinburgh City (despite the match having been moved to Easter Road!).

When Willie McCartney died and Hugh Shaw took over as manager at Easter Road, Kean gave up playing and became assistant trainer to Jimmy McColl, and he instilled a great sense of spirit among the squad, according to no less a judge than Lawrie Reilly.

'He was one of the great characters of the game and I personally never saw him in a bad mood,' recalled Reilly. 'He was a super character to have around on the training ground and every morning I couldn't get into training quick enough. He was a real bundle of fun.'

In the late 1950s, Kean moved to Dundee and went on to help coach Bob Shankly's championship-winning team of 1962. By 1965

Sammy was persuaded to take over the reins at Falkirk but his stint there was not a success and he moved on to resume coaching duties at Partick Thistle.
Appearances: 58 Goals: 0

KELLY Colin

A goalkeeper who joined Hibs briefly in season 1980/81 when Jim McArthur was injured. He played in two matches (against Ayr United and Motherwell) but Hibs, despite topping the First Division, lost the second of those games.
Appearances: 2 Goals: 0

KERR Jimmy

One of the bravest goalkeepers ever to serve Hibernian, Jimmy was signed by Willie McCartney in very unusual circumstance. He played as a fifteen-year-old in a schools match at Easter Road and was spotted from the stands. Thereafter he was loaned out to Ormiston Primrose in 1938 but his Hibs debut came while he was still only fifteen – against Chirnside United. Sadly his career was badly compromised by the war, but both before and after the hostilities, he shone.

Tall, strong and highly mobile Kerr was a fine 'keeper and a reassuring presence. During the war years Jimmy served in the RAF but managed to play first-team football when on leave and he was in the Hibees side that won the Summer Cup final against Rangers in 1941.

A plumber by trade, he played in what was quite clearly a different era. Quality players of his age like Bobby Nutley, Sammy Kean and Arthur Milne worked in the Leith shipyards during the war, while Davie Shaw was a miner and Tommy McIntyre worked away from football as a press photographer!

Jimmy Kerr's place in Hibernian folklore was assured when he saved a penalty from George Hamilton in the 1947 Scottish Cup final – but to no avail as Aberdeen won a Hampden Park thriller 2–1.

There was an element of irony in Kerr finally losing his place to understudy Tommy Younger. Both goalkeepers would eventually join the Board of Directors at Easter Road when Tom Hart was in charge of affairs!
Appearances: 72 Goals: 0

KILGOUR Rab

Initially on Meadowbank Thistle's staff, Rab reverted to non-League football with Whitehill Welfare before Hibernian signed him in 1978. He made his debut against Rangers at right-back just weeks later and impressed all with his composure. However, he rarely scaled those heights again and was destined to be a fringe player at Easter Road.

His short career at Hibs ended when he was granted a free transfer and he moved on to St Johnstone.
Appearances: 5 Goals: 0

KINLOCH Bobby

Broke into the Hibs side in the 1960/61 season and returned the most impressive figures of 10 goals in only 11 League matches. Considering that he also scored against Barcelona and Roma in our Fairs Cup adventures it was quite a season for Bobby. It was Bobby who converted arguably the most hotly disputed penalty in Hibs' long history when Barcelona contested an award in their 3–2 defeat at Easter Road that saw them ousted from Europe.

The following season he had only six League starts and it was clear that he was not going to be the answer to the post-Joe Baker era. He went to Greenock Morton in September 1962. From Scotland it was to Canada, where he played with Toronto City and Hamilton Steelers before the lure of his home country called and he joined Raith Rovers and then Dunfermline.
Appearances: 17 Goals: 12

KIRKWOOD Billy

But for a brief stint at Easter Road Billy Kirkwood would surely have been a one-club man – and that club would have been Dundee United. He joined the Tannadice outfit in 1976 and proved himself a versatile performer, rattling in 67 goals in almost 400 outings despite many of them being as a defender.

He won a Premier Division Championship badge in 1983 with United as well as two League Cup winner's medals. He moved to Hibernian in 1986 and made his debut in the 'Souness match'. Impressively strong and economical he was soon appointed club captain but his stay was short and he returned to Dundee United.

He later coached in the game and managed Hull City and Dundee United.
Appearances: 26 Goals: 1

L

LAING Dave

Dave had been capped twice while with Hearts before moving to Clyde. He won a Scottish Cup winner's badge as captain of Clyde. Thus when he joined Hibs in 1956 there was a degree of expectation. However, he was to play only six matches as a Hibee before moving on to Gillingham in August 1957.
Appearances: 6 Goals: 0

LAMBIE Duncan

Born in Whitburn in 1952, Duncan was a flying winger who joined Hibs in December 1978, having previously served Millwall, Dundee, St Johnstone and German club Furth.

Duncan made a most unusual Hibs debut, playing in the friendly at Tel Aviv in Israel.

His brother was John Lambie who as a player was a solid full-back and then as a coach began at Hibs before managing Partick Thistle and Hamilton.

Appearances: 17 Goals: 0

LARUSSON Bjarni

An Icelandic midfielder, Bjarnolfur made a sensational scoring debut for Hibs in a Premier League match at Kilmarnock. Coming on as a substitute he grabbed the Hibs goal in a 1–2 defeat.

He played in seven matches that season but as it ended in relegation it was a bad time to join the fray. Jim Duffy left the club and was replaced in the manager's office by Alex McLeish and Bjarni was never to feature in Alex's plans.

He was born in Iceland in 1976 and had been recruited from IBV Iceland.

Appearances: 7 Goals: 1

Bjarni Larusson.

LATAPY Russell

One of the most remarkably gifted players to serve Hibernian in the post-war era, Russell Latapy had all of the skills to justify his nick-name – 'Little Magician'.

He was raised on the Caribbean island of Trinidad and played with Trintoc, Port Morant United and the Newtown club in Port of Spain before being spotted while holidaying in Canada.

His progress once noticed was rapid. He joined Porto in 1995 and was farmed out to Portuguese Second Division side Academica Coimbra for four years. He had over 50 caps for Trinidad & Tobago before he moved to Portugal and by the time he retired from inter-national football had taken that total to over 100.

His stint on the Iberian peninsular reached its zenith with Porto and in Bobby Robson's side he was a UEFA Cup quarter-finalist and the first Trinidadian to play in the Champions League. From Porto he moved to city rivals Boavista, where he added a cup winner's medal to the two championship badges he had collected at Porto. More importantly for Hibernian, it brought him to Alex McLeish's attention.

Signed as a thirty-year-old during the club's successful First Division campaign of 1998/99 he quickly won a host of admirers. His trickery, powerful shooting and sheer entertainment value marked him out as the outstanding player – not only at Hibs – and he was duly voted First Division Player of the Year in 1999.

His wonderful, incisive play could open up the tightest of defences and in the modern era some of the finest Hibernian displays coincided with his 'good days'. Russell was one of the most popular sporting figures in the West Indies and his friend and West Indian cricket captain Brian Lara even came to Easter Road to cheer him on.

Russell Latapy with Brian Lara.

Many things made Russell such a good player. He could go past players with a mere shuffle of his feet or sway of his hips. His passing was incredibly perceptive and fell into the 'threading the needle' category. What's more he could, and did, score regularly, thumping shots in from all angles.

Sadly Russell's career at Hibernian ended in tawdry fashion. As the year 2001 got underway he was negotiating a new contract, which was seemingly too far from the club's budget. A late night drinking session in the spring saw him miss training. This was one indiscretion too many for the club and he did not play again for Hibs. Given that these events happened in the very season in which the club was chasing a Champions League spot and Scottish Cup glory this was truly unfortunate.

In the summer of 2001 Russell moved to Rangers, where he won a League Cup medal, before less successful stints with Dundee United and Falkirk.
Appearances: 82 Goals: 22

LAURSEN Ulrik

A Danish wing-back who always impressed with both his physique and his application. One of Alex McLeish's finest captures, the athletic Dane slotted into the Hibernian side with ease. Ulrik made his debut in the 0–0 draw with Hearts in July 2000 at Tynecastle and missed only a handful of games in his first season and even chipped in with a couple of League goals.

Capped 26 times by Denmark at Under-21 level, he was signed from OB Odense. Sadly his second season at the club was compromised by injury and when he returned to full fitness he left to join Celtic in a deal which the club could hardly refuse as a harsher economic climate swept through the game.
Appearances: 53 Goals: 3

LAVETY Barry

A £200,000 capture from St Mirren in August 1996, Barry scored on his debut against Brechin City. Alas, he was hit with a mystery virus soon afterwards and never seemed quite the same force again.

He did score the opening goal of Hibs' season in the First Division (a winner at Greenock) but was in and out of the team thereafter, even re-joining St Mirren on loan at one stage. He had a goal in a 2–1 win over Hearts during Alex McLeish's reign but his star was waning by then.

Eventually released, he returned to St Mirren but injury problems beset him and he was forced out of the game at a relatively early age. His first spell with St Mirren had been productive in that he scored 55 goals in 166 matches but was somewhat blighted by an off-the-field

Barry Lavety in action against Hearts.

problem. Between 1993 and 1995 he was capped nine times by Scotland at Under-21 level.

He re-emerged in the game via a study course spent at Bath University, whom he represented in the 2002/03 FA Cup.

Appearances: 66 Goals: 9

LEHMANN Dirk

A German striker, Dirk joined Hibernian in July 1999 and scored twice on his League debut against Motherwell. Very strong in the air, he nevertheless failed to score the number of goals his play often hinted at.

Dirk grabbed headlines in his early days at Hibs by virtue of wearing earrings, which he would cover up with huge elastoplasts on match day. The sight of him running around with large white squares hanging from his ears inevitably drew comments. However, he also earned column inches in the press for a few important counters in his time as a Hibs player. He netted in the 3–0 romp at Hearts in December 1999, and had two in a pulsating 5–2 win over Dundee at home in August 2000.

Dirk played 59 games for Hibs in the League (most of them as substitute) and scored 16 goals. He gradually slipped down the pecking order as the likes of Zitelli and Libbra came on board and moved to Brighton when he was unable to negotiate an extension to his contract.

Prior to playing for Hibs he had been with FC Energie Cottbus, RWD Molenbeek, Cologne and Fulham. He returned to

Dirk Lehmann.

Scotland from Brighton to join Motherwell and was at Fir Park during their financial turbulence of 2002.
Appearances: 59 Goals: 16

LEIGHTON Jim

Born in Johnstone in 1958, Jim Leighton is without doubt a member of the pantheon of great Scottish goalkeepers. His finest days may very well have come while keeping goal for Aberdeen but few would deny he made a huge impact while at Dundee and Hibernian. Moreover, he gave some legendary performances on the international stage.

He joined Aberdeen in 1977 and eventually flourished under Alex Ferguson, so much so that Fergie took him to Manchester United in a £750,000 deal in 1988. That transfer was a British record at the time.

He cemented his place as Scotland's number one goalkeeper while at Old Trafford until the fateful 1990 FA Cup final against Crystal Palace when his manager publicly blamed him for several mistakes.

He returned to Scotland and played with Dundee, who had bought him in early 1992 for £200,000, before Hibernian stepped in during the close season of 1993. Jim proved his reliability by being ever-present on League duty from 1993/94 through to 1995/96; indeed, he missed only one game in the 1996/97 campaign.

A veteran of the big occasion, he played in the 1993 League Cup final against Rangers and it took a quite outstanding overhead kick by Ally McCoist to beat him. Hibs would not have reached that final were it not for Jim saving no fewer than three spot kicks in a

Jim Leighton.

fourth-round penalty shoot out against Partick Thistle.

His final season at Easter Road was the 1996/97 campaign when the club had to defeat Airdrie in a play-off match to retain its Premier League status. Jim was off, back to Aberdeen, in the summer of 1997. Only Kenny Dalglish won more Scotland caps and Jim played in three World Cup finals (1986, 1990 and 1998).

Jim Leighton was made an MBE in the New Year Honours List of 1998.

Appearances: 151 Goals: 0

LEISHMAN Tom

Signed in January 1963 from Liverpool, Tom had played with St Mirren before moving to Anfield.

He scored his first goal for Hibs against Falkirk but thereafter failed to secure a regular place in the team for two and a half seasons.

After his time with Hibs was up he became player-manager of Linfield, the Belfast-based Irish side. He returned to Scotland in 1967 and spent a few seasons with Stranraer.

Appearances: 30 Goals: 1

LENNON Danny

Enjoyed a remarkably lengthy football career in Scotland and it is not unfair to say that Hibernian never really got the best from him.

He was one of a talented group of youngsters at the club in the late 1980s. Signed on an 'S' Form by John Blackley in 1985 while attached to Hutchison Vale BC, he established himself in the Hibernian reserve side before breaking into the first team. In seven seasons with Hibs he played 37 times.

He left Hibs for Raith Rovers and scored in their remarkable UEFA Cup clash with Bayern Munich. A full Northern Ireland international he got better as his career developed and probably reached his peak with Partick Thistle. In 2001 he was club captain as 'The

Jags' won the Second Division championship at a canter.

Born in Whitburn in 1969 he stood at 5ft 5in. Between his stints with Hibs and Partick Thistle he was playing with Ayr United and Ross County.

Appearances: 37 Goals: 2

LESLIE Lawrie

A reliable goalkeeper, Lawrie caught the eye of Hibernian when playing with Newtongrange Star and the Army. Manager Hugh Shaw signed him in 1956 and two years later the wisdom of that signing was apparent as Leslie gave an inspired display against Rangers in the Scottish Cup semi-final.

Generally he did well at Easter Road before moving to Airdrie in November 1959. Lawrie was captain for a spell at Broomfield. His exceptional form in the 1960/61 term earned him a move to West Ham United and he later played for Stoke and Millwall before completing his senior career at Southend.

Appearances: 76 Goals: 0

LIBBRA Marc

An exceptional centre forward, Alex McLeish brought this French striker to Hibs during the 2000/01 season. Tall and powerful he was also clever on the ground and scored some excellent goals for Hibs. Indeed, he scored on his debut at Celtic after coming off the bench.

In his short Hibs career he reserved many of his best showings for games against the Celts. He scored twice in our 2–5 defeat against them in 2001 and then gave the Glasgow side an early fright in the Scottish Cup final.

He was however only on loan to Hibs from Toulouse. Marc was with Marseilles as a youngster and then Cannes. Sadly in the summer of 2001 he was unable to secure a suitable deal at Hibernian and he joined English Division One side Norwich.

Marc Libbra.

He scored a stunning hat-trick in a pre-season friendly match for Norwich against Fakenham Town, then netted within 11 seconds of his full League debut against Manchester City. He could not sustain such heroics, however, and was released from his contract by Norwich in September 2002. In 2004 he joined Livingston from French football.
Appearances: 11 Goals: 5

LINWOOD Alex

Joined Hibernian in 1947 and won a Scottish League Championship medal in his very first season. However, for all Alex was a most talented forward, he was unable to command a regular spot, particularly when the 'Famous Five' began to gel. It was thus almost inevitable that Alex would move on and he duly joined Clyde in 1949.

Alexander Bryce Linwood began his senior career with St Mirren in 1939 and dominated their goalscoring tables throughout the war years. Indeed, he scored 148 goals for the Saints and netted their Summer Cup final winner against Rangers in 1943.

His goalscoring heroics earned him a move to Middlesbrough in June 1946 for £5,000 and it was from 'Boro that Hibs bought the lively striker. He was a prolific marksman but certainly upstaged. The 8–0 win over Third Lanark in November 1947 was a point in case. He scored a hat-trick that day, but it was uncommented on because Gordon Smith scored the other five goals!

From Hibs he moved to Clyde and then on to Morton, and he served the Greenock club from 1951 to 1955.

Alex Linwood.

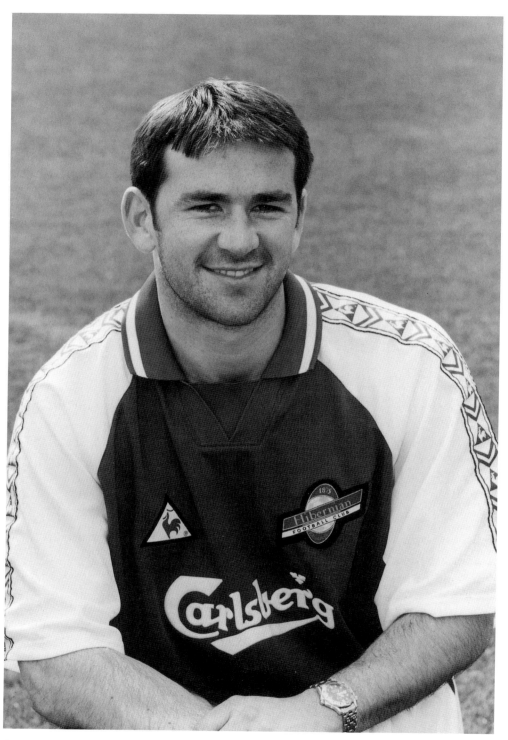

Stuart Lovell.

While with the Bully Wee he played in the 1949 Scottish Cup final. That was also the year in which he gained his only Scotland cap, scoring against Wales in a 2–0 win.

Appearances: 36 Goals: 22

LOVE Graeme

Born in Bathgate in December 1973, Graeme spent six years as a Hibee and, between 1991 and 1997, made 39 League appearances. He never managed more than a dozen or so games in any one season so it is probably fair to say that this strong tackling defender was something of a fringe player.

He moved to Ayr United in the summer of 1997 and his full-back talents were put to use there until he moved on to Queen of the South then Clydebank.

When junior football began its Premier League in 2002, Graeme was in the Bathgate side that took part.

Appearances: 39 Goals: 0

LOVELL Stuart

Signed by Alex McLeish when Hibernian dropped into the First Division, Lovell was an outstanding success and arguably underrated by many. He came to Hibs having scored 67 goals in 150 matches for Reading and matched his prowess with industry.

An eloquent speaker on the game, he provided graft in a midfield boasting players such as Latapy and Sauzee and helped the club not only achieve promotion but contributed several quality goals from a midfield position. His finest was surely a curling effort against St Johnstone from the edge of the area as Hibs consolidated in the top flight.

A member of the Hibernian Scottish Cup final team, he was rather surprisingly allowed to leave in the summer of 2001 and joined a thriving Livingston – where he proved his worth rather quickly. In 2004 he was captain of the Livingston side that beat Hibs 2–0 in the CIS Cup final… irony indeed!

Appearances: 85 Goals: 17

LOVERING Paul

Signed by Alex McLeish from Clydebank in October 1998, Paul was a left-back with prodigious talent in the air. Clydebank had farmed him out to Neilston Juniors and then used him from March 1995 onwards. He was Second Division Player of the Year and a promotion winner with the Bankies.

His career with Hibernian started well and his phenomenal heading ability caught the eye. However, he failed to build upon a solid start and let the team down badly when sent off along with Franck Sauzee in a 0–2 Easter Road reversal to Celtic in September 1999. Eventually Paul was allowed to join Ayr United. He had the last laugh, playing for Ayr in the shock League Cup semi-final victory they achieved over Hibernian in 2001.

Appearances: 22 Goals: 1

LUNA Francisco Javier Aguilera Blanco

'Paco' Luna joined Hibernian from Mexican side Monterray in 2001. A Spanish born centre forward, he had played at the highest level in Spain with Sporting Gijon and with lesser lights Almeria and Albacete. In March 2000 he had a short stint with Dundee and it was while at Dens that Hibs boss Alex McLeish had seen him.

He was a clever forward and, while not the tallest, he was excellent in the air. When Hibernian met AEK Athens in the UEFA Cup he almost won the tie for Hibs, scoring twice in regulation time and going ever so close in the final seconds to securing what would have been a stunning win.

Paco returned to Almeria in the early part of 2003.

Appearances: 43 Goals: 8

Paco Luna in action against Alloa.

M

MacFARLANE Willie

One of that select band of Hibernian players who returned to manage the club. His father had played for Leith and St Bernards, so Willie was of good footballing stock.

He was signed in 1949 by Hugh Shaw and learned his trade with Hutcheson Vale and Tranent before making his debut in a friendly against Tottenham Hotspur. He played in the great European nights that saw Hibs reach the European Cup semi-finals.

In 1953 Willie joined Raith Rovers but soon afterwards moved to Morton with Hal Stewart. From there it was into management, a career that began in the humble surrounds of Gala then carried him to Hawick and Stirling Albion.

He was a part-time manager at Stirling, working during the days as a plant-transport manager and concentrating on Albion in the evenings. However, when Bob Shankly left Hibs, Willie was invited to concentrate solely on football as Easter Road boss. One of his first acts was to bring young Stirling defender Erich Schaedler to Easter Road.

Willie made a good start at Hibs, including a win at Tynecastle but he was to last just over a year and when chairman Tom Hart began to contemplate bringing Eddie Turnbull to Hibs as manager it was clear that Willie's time was coming to an end.

Appearances: 78 Goals: 2

MacLEOD Ally (1)

Born in Glasgow on 26 February 1931, Alistair Reid MacLeod was destined to be one of the biggest figures in the history of Scottish football.

This particular Ally (for there were two who served Hibs) was to earn enormous fame, and indeed affection, as manager of Scotland. His was a colourful career that encompassed spells in club management with Motherwell, Airdrie, Queen of the South, Aberdeen and, most popularly, Ayr United. As a player he served Third Lanark, St Mirren, Hibernian and Blackburn.

Ally was born on the south side of Glasgow in February 1931 and as a boy was a fanatical Third Lanark supporter. How appropriate then that his playing career began with Third Lanark before it carried him to St Mirren, where he impressed sufficiently to earn a move to England with Blackburn. He was an FA Cup finalist with Rovers and served them from 1956 to 1960.

From Rovers he came to Hibs in July 1961. He impressed with his shrewd ability and was noticeable by dint of his leggy style. However, he was in the veteran stages and only lasted a couple of years as a Hibee before making a sentimental return to Third Lanark.

It was to be as a manager that he really caught the eye. He took Ayr United to new heights in a ten-year spell that propelled Ayr from obscurity to a regular diet of Premier League soccer. Having steered United to promotion, his first game in the top league was against Hibs and his team showed little respect for a club who included quality players like Pat Stanton, Jim O'Rourke and Joe McBride. A 3–0 victory, a bumper crowd on a hot Sunday in August and Ally and his team had well and truly arrived.

From Ayr his journey to being Scotland manager was via Aberdeen. What is often forgotten in the aftermath of the Argentina World Cup fiasco of 1978 is that Ally rallied a footballing nation like no Scotland boss did before or after.

There was an interesting postscript to Ally's football career. While boss of Queen of the South he played a match on 14 April 1992 as a sixty-one-year-old. The game was a reserve match against St Mirren that the Paisley club won 8–1… but Ally scored the visitors' goal with a penalty!

Appearances: 52 Goals: 6

MacLEOD Ally (2)

A fairly sensational young striker with St Mirren, he served notice of his ability by scoring all four Saints goals in a 4–1 win at Rangers. That earned him a move to Southampton but he failed to settle on the South Coast.

In December 1974 Hibs signed him and in so doing completed one of their sharpest pieces of business. He went on to play over 300 games as a Hibee and was a prolific marksman in the modern 'defensively coached' era.

Ally MacLeod

His debut came in a goalless draw at Airdrie in December 1974.

In the season that Hearts were relegated for the first time in their history; MacLeod scored a vital derby winner and his glut of goals late in the season ensured Hibs did not go down. He was also on target in the 1979 Scottish Cup final when Hibs lost to Rangers, but only after two replays.

Appearances: 208 Goals: 72

MacLEOD John

Born in Edinburgh in 1938, John joined Hibernian after a spell with Armadale Thistle and he made a stunning debut in 1957 as Hibs won 4–1 at Kilmarnock and laid to rest a twenty-year bogey at Rugby Park.

His early career went well and a hat-trick in a 10–2 away win at Partick Thistle suggested he was likely to be a first-team player for some time to come. He was capped at Under-23 level but was unfortunate to be in the full Scotland side massacred 9–3 at Wembley in 1961 (Pat Quinn also played in this debacle).

He scored 27 goals in 85 League games before electing to try his luck down south. John moved to George Swindin's Arsenal in July 1961 but the pace that had served him so well in Scotland was less effective in the top English league. That said he did score the first Arsenal goal in European football. From Arsenal, where he scored 23 goals in 101 League games, he moved to Aston Villa and was with them from 1964 through to 1967. His final port of call was Belgium with KV Mechelen. He completed his senior career with a stint at Raith Rovers in season 1971/72.

A very tidy player, John was perhaps underrated in his time at Easter Road and his century plus of outings for both Arsenal and Aston Villa suggests a quality performer.

Appearances: 86 Goals: 28

MacLEOD Murdo

A product of Glasgow amateur football, Murdo joined Dumbarton in 1974 and had four years with the Boghead side before moving to Celtic in November 1978 for a fee of £100,000. His stay at Parkhead was highly successful, picking up four League Championship medals, two Scottish Cup winner's medals and one League Cup winner's badge. He gained Under-21 and full caps for Scotland while at Parkhead.

A battling midfielder, he was known for the power and accuracy of his long range shooting and he used this to good effect for Celtic and Scotland.

The Scotland caps continued when he had a spell in Germany with Borussia Dortmund. Joining in the summer of 1987, he won a German Cup medal – and duly became the first Scot to do so.

He returned to Scotland with Hibs in October 1990 and promptly won a League Cup winner's badge in 1991. He later entered coaching and made his mark with Dumbarton, Partick Thistle and Celtic, serving under Wim Jansen at Parkhead. He then went into the media, working as a pundit for BBC Scotland.

Appearances: 78 Goals: 2

MADSEN John

A Danish international centre half, John was signed from Morton in July 1966. His early performances were said by some to be compromised by his insistence on staying in Greenock and travelling by train to Edinburgh. However, a move to Barnton soon settled him.

He returned to Denmark in the summer of 1968 to resume his career as an architect. However, he was still under contract to Hibs and returned to Easter Road in the autumn (had he not he would have been banned *sine die* by the SFA).

Murdo MacLeod, an engaging personality both on and off the field.

John Madsen.

Peter Marinello.

Robust and resolute, he was well liked by the Hibernian support.
Appearances: 71 Goals: 0

MARINELLO Peter

Born in Edinburgh in February 1950, he joined Hibs in 1966 from Salveson BC. By the time he had reached eighteen he was a first-team regular. In little over two seasons he made 45 League outings for Hibs and chipped in with 5 goals. A dashing winger, he was light but tricky and hard to contain.

The 1969/70 season saw him reach his peak at Easter Road and he scored twice in an impressive 3–1 win over Rangers. It was not just Hibs that thought he looked good, Arsenal did too and in January 1970 they signed him for £100,000.

With his long dark hair, good looks and youthful wing skills he was rather unfortunately compared to George Best. Arriving in London he was saddled with this impossible comparison but scored a dazzling goal on his debut at Old Trafford. However, 5 goals in 51 matches was not good enough for the Gunners and his career went into decline.

He followed his Highbury days with spells at Portsmouth, Motherwell, Fulham, Phoenix Inferno and, in a return to Edinburgh, Hearts. He called a halt to his career while at Partick Thistle.

Off the field Peter once presented BBC's iconic music programme *Top of the Pops* and he starred in a national milk advert.
Appearances: 42 Goals: 5

MARINKOV Alex

Born in 1967 in the French town of Grenoble, Marinkov was signed by Alex McLeish as Hibs stormed towards promotion. He played his part (9 games and 1 goal) but left early the following season to revert to playing amateur football in France.

In France Marinkov had played with Annency, Martigue, Limoges and Raon L'Etape. He then tried his luck in England with Scarborough before joining Hibernian, but the feeling was that Alex did not relish being a full-time footballer and preferred the part-time option.
Appearances: 9 Goals: 1

MARJORIBANKS Brian

A forward, he played in 5 League matches in the 1961/62 season. He had joined the Hibees from Airth Castle Rovers.

Appearances: 5 Goals: 3

MARSHALL Gordon

Few Hibs players have endured such an inauspicious start to their careers as Gordon Marshall. A highly rated goalkeeper, he conceded two goals within six minutes of his debut against St Johnstone in Perth.

Bob Shankly signed him in 1969 after he had earned a Scotland Under-23 cap and played with Hearts, Newcastle and Nottingham Forest. Indeed, he had won League and League Cup winner's medals while at Tynecastle, so it was clear that he knew his stuff.

After leaving Hibs he joined Celtic, Aberdeen and then Arbroath. His son (also called Gordon) became a noted goalkeeper

Gordon Marshall.

too, playing with the likes of Kilmarnock and Celtic.

Appearances: 47 Goals: 0

MARTIN Lilian

Signed by Franck Sauzee, shortly before the termination of his appointment, Lilian enters the category reserved for 'one-game' wonders. A skilled French full-back, his solitary outing came in a 1–1 draw with Dunfermline.

Lilian was thirty when he joined Hibs and had starred for Marseille, Monaco and Derby County.

Appearances: 1 Goals: 0

MARTIN Neil

Signed from Queen of the South in 1963 for £6,000, Martin had been raised in Tranent and relished joining Hibs. Prior to playing with Queen of the South he had been at Alloa and had gained renown for his heading ability and eye for goal.

He proved a great signing for Hibs, netting goals with some gusto. His record of 53 League goals from only 65 matches between 1963 and 1966 is nothing short of superb. It is probably fair to say that he was unlucky that the only trophy we won during his stint at Hibs was the Summer Cup.

In season 1963/64 he bagged 20 goals in just 28 League starts and he had 25 from 31 in the next season as Hibs reached the Scottish Cup semi-final and began to look like a very good side indeed. He had helped the club reach the League Cup semi-finals with 9 goals and also had 8 League strikes in only 6 matches when he was lured away.

Neil was sold to Sunderland in October 1965 for £45,000, which represented a considerable profit on our outlay. He was an instant hit on Wearside and scored 38 goals in 86 matches for the Rokerites before moving to Coventry and Nottingham Forest – where he was equally prolific. He later played with

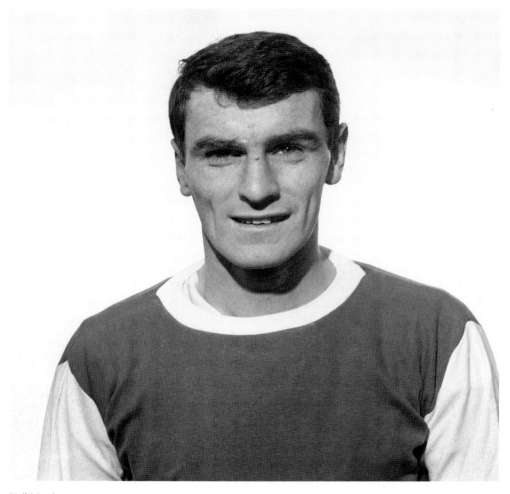

Neil Martin.

Brighton and Crystal Palace before coaching Al-Arabi Sporting Club of Kuwait and could reflect on a career that brought three Scotland caps.

He scored 100 League goals in Scotland and repeated that feat in England; few achieve that notable double.

Appearances: 65 Goals: 53

MATHISEN Svein

One of two Norwegian players signed in trying circumstances in 1978, Svein always appeared more likely to stay with Hibernian as he was a full international and therefore more likely to acquire the, then, essential Department of Employment clearance. Svein had actually played for Norway against Scotland in a European Nations Cup match and held seven caps. He made his debut, along with Isak Refvik, against Morton in a dramatic League Cup quarter-final tie.

He was born in Kristiansen in 1952 and, as well as his 7 full caps, had 8 Under-23 caps. He was a teacher and signed from IFK Start.

Appearances: 2 Goals: 0

MATYUS Janos

A Hungarian wing-back Janos was signed by Bobby Williamson early in the 2002/03 season when Hibs endured a wretched start to the season.

He had won 30 Hungarian Under-23 caps and 34 senior caps so was clearly a quality performer. Indeed, he had actually played at Easter Road in 1996 for Hungary Under-23s.

His previous clubs had included Honved, Ferencvaros and Energie Cottbus. He fitted in well at Hibs and was a steady performer but, alas, he was in the veteran stages and lasted just a single year before returning to Hungary.
Appearances: 14 Goals: 0

MAY Eddie

Eddie left Dundee United (he was homesick) to join Hibernian in 1985. A versatile little player he was with Hibs until 1989 and in that time made 109 League appearances.

He was a sprightly and direct player, capable of playing as a scoring midfielder or a defensive full-back. His versatility made him a regular first-team choice.

He was badly missed when he moved to Brentford in a deal worth £165,000. Although he returned to Scotland fairly quickly, it was to Falkirk not Edinburgh.

From Brockville, where by his own admission he played his best football, he moved to Motherwell then Dunfermline.
Appearances: 109 Goals: 10

McALLISTER Kevin

The archetypal Scottish winger, standing at 5ft 5in, who provided marvellous entertainment throughout his lengthy career.

Kevin's football odyssey began when he went from Camelon Juniors to Falkirk in 1983. He was a huge hit at the club he supported and was snapped up by Chelsea for £34,000

Janos Matyus.

101

Kevin McAllister.

in June 1985. Six years at Stamford Bridge followed, the highlights of which were arguably featuring in two winning sides at Wembley in the Full Members and Zenith Data cup finals.

In August 1991 Kevin returned to Brockville as the then Falkirk manager Jim Jefferies convinced the Brockville board to spend a club record fee of £225,000.

An entertaining Falkirk side slipped out of the Premier League in the summer of 1993 and, being financially pressed, they had little hesitation in accepting a £235,000 offer for Kevin from Hibs boss Alex Miller. It was one of Alex's most shrewd purchases and with McAllister on one wing and Michael O'Neill on the other Hibs regained much of their traditional flair. Kevin proved a darling of the terraces with his trickery and bravery and it is no coincidence that his time at Easter Road saw Hibs reach the 1993 League Cup final.

Ten days after the arrival of Jim Duffy as Hibs' boss, Kevin was on his way back to Falkirk in a £25,000 deal. He reached a Scottish Cup final with the Bairns and won a Challenge Cup medal in what proved a fairly prolonged Indian summer to his career. Throughout, the enduring quality Kevin brought to the game was entertainment value. In 2002 he joined Albion Rovers in order to take up a player/coach post.
Appearances: 109 Goals: 12

McARTHUR Jim

A goalkeeper of considerable talent, Jim joined Hibs in 1972 from Cowdenbeath for £8,000. He made his debut against Dumbarton a few months later but had to be patient and spent some time on the sidelines watching Mike McDonald put together an impressive run of outings.

Patience they say is a virtue and Jim proved the theory. When he had finally won the first-team jersey he held on to it for the most part until 1983. That allowed him to

Jim McArthur.

clock up over 200 appearances as a Hibee and such loyalty was rewarded by a testimonial against Hearts.

A modest player, he attributed much of his success to good defences in front of him – Brownlie, Blackley, Black and Schaedler then Bremner, McNamara and Stewart – but the truth is he was a very capable performer.

Away from football he was a physical education instructor but he later became a football agent and was often seen at Easter Road in a professional capacity.
Appearances: 217 Goals: 0

McBRIDE Joe (junior)

The son of the former Hibernian and Celtic striker of the same name, Joe junior was a tricky winger. Born in Glasgow in 1960, he went from school straight to Everton, where he truly impressed. He scored on his debut against Bolton and benefited from playing alongside quality players of the calibre of Kidd, Hartford and Latchford.

From Everton it was on to Rotherham United then Oldham Athletic. Joe joined Hibernian from Oldham in 1985, signed by John Blackley who memorably quipped: 'I played with the father and now I have signed the son!'

He settled well at Easter Road and was a goal-taker as well as a goal-provider. Pride of place must surely go to his performance in the April 1985 derby at Tynecastle, when he had both Hibs goals in a 2–2 draw.

Joe stayed at Easter Road until 1988 when he moved to Hamilton Accies. From Douglas Park it was on to a brief spell in the juniors with Maryhill.

Appearances: 81 Goals: 10

McBRIDE Joe (senior)

One of the most prolific strikers in post-war Scottish football, Joe's career was both nomadic and exciting. Born in Govan, just 200 yards from Ibrox Park, he joined Kilmarnock when he was fifteen and was loaned out to Kirkintilloch Rob Roy. When he returned to Killie he was an instant hit and was sold for the then considerable sum of £12,500 to Wolves.

Unable to make his mark at Wolves, he journeyed south to Luton and from there he joined Partick Thistle but it was his next move – to Motherwell – that really kick-started his career.

He was a spectacular goalscorer for Motherwell. Although just 5ft 8in he was strong in the air but it was on the ground that he really made his mark and his power – allied to razor sharp instincts around goal – made him a feared opponent.

In 1963, 1964 and 1965 he was top scorer for Motherwell and he helped the 'Well knock Hibs out of the 1965 Summer Cup semi-finals. Jock Stein noted his prowess and signed him for Celtic in a £22,000 deal in 1965.

He stayed at Parkhead until 1968 and in that time won all the domestic honours. Clearly he would have been a Lisbon Lion but for picking up an injury in December of the 1966/67 season. Nevertheless, he was still top scorer in the division, having netted 35 goals in 26 starts when injury struck.

Hibs signed Joe in 1968 and he quickly settled into the scoring routine. There was a goal on his League debut against Rangers, a hattrick against Leipzig in the very next match, and four in his next outing – against Morton. Little wonder that within a week of signing he was a cult hero on the terraces.

Mind you, we did know what to expect from Joe. He had scored all four Celtic goals in a 4–3 win at Easter Road in October 1966.

Nineteen goals in 23 matches in his first League season was an awesome return. He hit the 20 mark in the next season. Between 1968 and 1971 Joe was to play 66 League games for Hibs and score a very respectable 44 goals.

There was frustration and anger when he was allowed to move to Dunfermline and he ended his senior career in the colours of Clyde. He later revealed to me that he had been forced out at Hibs because he refused to move home from Glasgow to Edinburgh.

Appearances: 66 Goals: 44

McCABE Thomas

Signed from Douglas Water Primrose and a miner by trade, Thomas found first-team openings very limited at Easter Road. Indeed, in September 1948 he was moved on loan to Hamilton having played 13 games in the first season after the war for Hibs. His senior career ended with a stint at Falkirk.

Appearances: 13 Goals: 0

McCAFFREY Stuart

Stuart made only a handful of outings for Hibernian before moving to Aberdeen in the summer of 1999. His transfer was settled by a tribunal, with Aberdeen being required to pay £60,000 when Hibernian had asked for £100,000 compared to the Dons' £37,500 valuation. He never made the expected progress at Pittodrie and drifted to Inverness Caledonian Thistle.

Appearances: 2 Goals: 0

McCLELLAND Joe

The Hibs groundsman in the late 1950s, Harry Reading, ran a club called Edinburgh Thistle and it was from this nursery club that Hibs recruited many of their players. Joe McClelland was one such signing. Born in Edinburgh in 1935, he may have been a late starter but Joe was worth the wait.

He played twice in the 1955/56 season and by season 1957/58 was established at left-back and played in the disappointing 1958 Scottish Cup final defeat against Clyde. Away from Easter Road he was an industrious lad and coached the Americans who wanted to play soccer at the US air base in Kirknewton, Edinburgh.

In June 1964 Joe joined Wrexham but he came back to Scotland to coach Armadale and Ferranti Thistle. Away from football he earned his living working in a bakery!

Appearances: 183 Goals: 2

McCLUSKEY George

It was John Blackley who signed George from Leeds United in 1986. The clever striker had spent three years at Elland Road but made his name at Celtic, with whom he won all the major Scottish domestic honours. He spent eight seasons at Celtic and scored 52 League goals for them, before rattling in 16 goals in 73 League outings for Leeds.

A former Under-21 international, he continued to score for Hibs in a five-year career at Easter Road. George is well remembered as the victim of 'that tackle' by Graeme Souness

George McCluskey.

in a particularly tempestuous clash with Rangers at Easter Road in 1986.

He left for Hamilton after a three-year spell with Hibs and cost the Lanarkshire club £35,000. His stint at Hamilton saw him reunited with Colin Harris, with whom he had shared attacking duties at Hibs. George later played with Kilmarnock and Clyde.

Appearances: 83 Goals: 15

McCLUSKIE Jamie

If ever evidence was needed that Hibernian was a club totally committed to its youth policy in the early part of the new millennium, then it came in the winter of 2003 at Kilmarnock. A Hibs side ravaged by injury (Brebner, Glass, Murray and Thomson were all ruled out) was forced to list the sixteen-year-old McCluskey as a substitute and the young man made his debut in the 84th

minute. His claim to fame was being the youngest Hibee in forty years.
Appearances: 1 Goals: 0

McCREADIE Thomas

Born in Johnstone in 1943, this talented full-back scored three times for Hibs in the 1962/63 season but fancied his chances south of the border. He joined Watford in 1963 but made only one League outing for the Hornets.
Appearances: 9 Goals: 3

McCURDY Pat

The offer of a contract at Hibs was enough for the Greenock youngster to abandon his painting and decorating apprenticeship in 1982. He was rewarded quickly as he scored on his debut for Hibs in an 8–1 rout of Kilmarnock in April 1983. He played his last game in the 1983/84 season having failed to make a more lasting impression.

In 1984 he became a member of John Lambie's Hamilton Accies squad but his left-wing talents did not really blossom there either. Subsequent moves carried him to Morton, Stranraer and Alloa.

He enjoyed greater success in the junior ranks, serving Dalry Thistle and then netting the winner in the 1994 Scottish Junior Cup final for Largs Thistle (Alan Rough was in the opposition dug-out as Glenafton manager).
Appearances: 5 Goals: 1

McDONALD Kevin

Signed from Sunderland in 2003, young Kevin was integrated into the Hibernian youth system and made his bow on the final day of the 2003/04 season. A midfielder, he was born in Newcastle.
Appearances: 1 Goals: 0

McDONALD Mike

A solid goalkeeper, Mike arrived at Easter Road intent on fulfilling his promise. Born in

Mike McDonald.

Glasgow he had started his career with Clydebank shortly after the club entered the Scottish League in 1965. Mike was 'a Bankie' for five years before moving on to Stoke City where he was apprentice not just to Gordon Banks but also Peter Shilton. Not surprisingly, first-team openings were limited!

Eddie Turnbull signed Mike for Hibs for £25,000 in January 1976 and this soon proved to be money well spent. He played in over 100 League games for Hibs and showed himself to be an able shot stopper.

There was, however, one bitter disappointment. In the League Cup semi-final of 1978 against Aberdeen he was beaten by a long distance lob from Stewart Kennedy after 107 minutes of a tense game at Dens Park.

After leaving Easter Road he played with Dundee and Berwick before making the short journey to Tynecastle in order to coach Hearts reserves. However, the game still pulled at him and he returned to playing with Hawick and then St Johnstone.
Appearances: 109 Goals: 0

McDONALD Tommy

A talented outside left, Tommy was born in Glasgow in May 1930 and joined Hibs in the late 1940s. He made his League debut in the 1949/50 season, and scored his first League goals in the 1953/54 season when he grabbed 6 in 14 games.

Ultimately he was unable to command a regular first-team spot. He signed for Wolverhampton Wanderers in April 1954 but played only five games before moving on to Leicester City, where he enjoyed three very successful seasons and scored 27 goals in only 113 matches.

In 1960, aged thirty, he signed for Dunfermline and he was able to help them reach the 1961 Scottish Cup final. Sadly he missed the final through injury and a couple of years later he joined Raith Rovers.
Appearances: 16 Goals: 6

McEWAN Billy

Signed in 1967 from Uphall Saints, Billy was essentially a fringe player at Hibs. A half-back, he found it hard to cement a regular first-team spot but did celebrate scoring a European winner against Mälmo. Overall he had 61 League outings to his name between 1969 and 1973.

He later played in England with the likes of Blackpool, Brighton, Chesterfield, Mansfield, Peterborough and Rotherham.
Appearances: 61 Goals: 2

McGACHIE John

Signed by Hibs from Aberdeen in 1984, John was a Scotland Schoolboy international. He did not make the expected impact at Easter Road and moved on to Hamilton Accies having made just 11 outings for Hibs. He did score a notable counter against Aberdeen at the tail end of the 1983/84 season.

He netted on his debut for Accies and proved a useful marksman for them before he joined Meadowbank for one year. Thereafter he returned to Hamilton before serving Stirling Albion, Montrose and Keith.
Appearances: 11 Goals: 1

McGHEE Alex

A forward, he played with Hibs in the late 1970s. Between 1971 and 1978 he played 25 matches for the club, which confirmed his fringe status. He was transferred to Dundee in 1978.
Appearances: 25 Goals: 6

McGINLAY Pat

Born in Glasgow in 1967, Pat went from Anniesland Waverely to Blackpool when only seventeen. He was there for three seasons before moving to Hibs in 1983 and beginning a long association with the club.

A very versatile player, he was happiest in midfield but his goals-to-games ratio suggested

Pat McGinlay.

he could have played as a forward with ease. He was a League Cup winner with Hibs in 1991 and was on the verge of international honours when Celtic signed him for £525,000 in 1993.

A consistent marksman for the Celts, he nevertheless did not quite seem to fit and Hibs were able to lure him back in November 1994 for a club record fee of £425,000.

He came into his own after Hibs were relegated in 1998 and helped the club achieve promotion with a dozen goals. He left the club soon afterwards to join Ayr United.

Appearances: 322 Goals: 60

McGLINCHEY Paul

An Edinburgh-born midfielder, Paul joined Hibs from Tynecastle Boys Club in 1978. He struggled to impress himself on the first-team scene and by 1980 had had managed only seven League appearances.

A silk-screen printer by trade, his stay at Easter Road was short but he did manage an outing for Scotland's Professional Youth side while a Hibee.

Appearances: 15 Goals: 0

McGLYNN Tony

An inside forward, Tony was signed from Edinburgh Thistle in 1961. He scored the winner against Raith Rovers early in the 1961/62 season but that was the only occasion on which his services were called upon that term.

Two seasons later he found the target against Motherwell but failed to hold his place in the first team. He left Hibs in 1964 having scored twice in his three outings.

Appearances: 3 Goals: 2

McGOVERN Paul

Edinburgh-born Paul joined Hibernian as a seventeen-year-old from Royston Rosebery in 1985. He made his debut for the first team in a 3–2 Skol Cup win over Montrose.

He was to play only six games for Hibernian, and five of those saw him start from the bench. His career later took in Partick Thistle and Gala Fairydean as well as a spell in Cyprus.

Appearances: 6 Goals: 1

McGRAW Allan

A superb striker with Morton, it was rather unfortunate that Hibs did not sign Allan until 1966. By that stage he was already being plagued by the knee injuries that would ultimately end his career.

His career with Morton was so good that it merits retelling even in a publication essentially about Hibs. Such was the prolific nature of McGraw's scoring he earned the soubriquet 'Quick Draw' McGraw. He once scored over 50 goals in a season for Morton and twice helped the club gain promotion, as well as reach the 1963 League Cup final.

He was five seasons with Morton and their top scorer in each and every one. In the League Cup semi-final of 1963 he scored the goal that denied Hibs a final place at the expense of the Greenock club.

As a Hibs player McGraw, while hampered by injury, looked every bit the complete professional. His commitment was beyond reproach and while not as prolific as he had been at Cappielow he was a useful goalscorer. In 1968 he scored a League Cup semi-final winner against Dundee that entered Easter Road folklore. The circumstances were unusual in that he was effectively a lame duck at the time, having been badly injured but remaining on the field as Hibs had already used their only substitute (Jim O'Rourke). Helped into the penalty area when Hibs earned a late corner, he responded by poking home the winner from close range.

From Hibs he moved very briefly to Linfield in Northern Ireland and then back to Morton. There he began a coaching career that saw

Allan McGraw.

him manage the Greenock club with some distinction.

One of the finest gentlemen of the game, Allan is a hero in Greenock – deservedly so!
Appearances: 60 Goals: 17

McGRAW Mark

Son of Allan McGraw, the ex Hibs and Morton striker, Mark began his senior career at Cappielow while his father was the boss. He had played only a handful of matches for Morton when Alex Miller signed him for Hibs in February 1990.

He tore ankle ligaments not long into his Hibs career and was arguably never the same player again. After his five-year stint with Hibs, which brought 49 League games, he turned out for several smaller clubs, including Falkirk and Clyde.
Appearances: 49 Goals: 3

McGURK Dennis

A Dundonian, Dennis joined Hibernian from Dunkeld Amateurs and was from footballing stock – his father having played with

Portadown. However, young Dennis struggled to break through at Easter Road and was restricted to a single outing in the 1949/50 season.
Appearances: 1 Goals: 0

McINTOSH Martin

The early part of Martin's career was spent with Hamilton Accies and St Mirren. When Martin had gone to Stockport County in England he had earned Hamilton Accies £80,000. A tall, powerful and aggressive centre half, he caught the eye and clearly Alex McLeish had been impressed, for he wasted no time in luring Martin back to Scotland when the opportunity arose.

He played nine matches in the 1999/2000 season but seemed to fall from favour fairly quickly. Four games were all he could manage the following season before he departed for Rotherham United.
Appearances: 13 Goals: 0

McINTYRE Tommy

A scorer in the 1991 League Cup final triumph, Tommy joined Hibs in December 1986 from Aberdeen. A towering centre half, he was good value at £30,000. He scored six League goals in that 1991/92 season and was probably at his peak that term. In all, Tommy played 126 League games for Hibs.
Appearances: 126 Goals: 9

McKAY Jim

Signed on a one-month loan deal from Highland League club Brora Rangers in 1977, his debut came against Newcastle United in a 3–0 friendly win. He worked in a mill back in the Highlands.
Appearances: 4 Goals: 1

McKEE Kevin

A clever young full-back, Kevin joined Hibs in 1982, having played with Whitburn and

Polbeth. He made his bow in May 1983 while still only sixteen and began to impress all and sundry with his speed of thought and neat distribution.

However, openings were limited at Easter Road and he moved on to Hamilton, where he won League and cup medals. Later in his career he moved to Glasgow with Partick Thistle then on to Stenhousemuir.

His spell as a Hibs player is perhaps, and unfortunately often, associated with an attack he suffered on the pitch at Ibrox from a drunken Rangers supporter. Kevin played 37 League games for Hibs.

Appearances: 37 Goals: 0

McKENZIE Roddy

Goalkeeper Roddy McKenzie was signed by Hibernian as an emergency cover in August 1973. With regular 'keeper Jim McArthur ruled out with a broken bone in his hand and young Bobby Robinson deemed too inexperienced, manager Eddie Turnbull went into the transfer market and recruited Roddy.

A twenty-seven-year-old Irish international (he had been capped against Wales in 1967) he was in dispute with Airdrie and thus easily recruited. Alas, his debut was fairly traumatic as he blundered in a 1–4 reversal at Dumbarton. He did however recover and went on to make seven appearances for Hibs in the 1973/74 season before McArthur returned.

Roddy had been with Airdrie for a decade, joining them from Drumchapel Amateurs. From Hibernian he moved to Clydebank.

Appearances: 7 Goals: 0

McLAREN Billy

Joined Hibs in December 1980 from Morton and helped the club regain Premier League status. A rugged defender, he took few prisoners but there was more to his game than brawn and he displayed this by enjoying a lengthy coaching career after quitting playing.

Prior to joining Hibs Billy had played with Kirkintilloch Rob Roy, Dunfermline, Raith, East Fife, and Queen of the South.

Never a full-time player, he was a civil servant and as such determined to avoid the potential pitfalls of fully professional football.

Appearances: 38 Goals: 0

McLAUGHLIN Joe

Joe McLaughlin was a towering and clever centre-back whose career was able to outlast most of his contemporaries by virtue of his dedication. He made his breakthrough in the 1970s with Greenock Morton, winning 10 Under-21 caps, and was a big buy for Chelsea. After six seasons at Stamford Bridge he moved to Watford and then Charlton before coming back to Scotland.

He was with Falkirk when Hibs swooped in 1995. In essence he was an emergency signing for Hibernian and viewed as cover in a difficult period. He was a Hibee from 1995 to 1997 and played 18 times on League duty.

Appearances: 18 Goals: 0

McMANUS Michael

A teenager when he made his only outing for Hibernian as a substitute, he replaced Ralph Callachan in a disappointing fixture at St Mirren in December 1984. Hibs lost the game 2–3 after young goalkeeper Robin Rae made a dreadful hash of the second goal.

Appearances: 1 Goals: 0

McMANUS Tom

Born in Glasgow in 1981, 'Tam' joined Hibs straight from school and his pacy, snappy, style of forward play made him a favourite with the Easter Road support.

He had loan spells with Airdrie and East Fife, scoring 3 times in 11 games for the latter before really making his mark at Hibs. His Scottish Cup quarter-final winner at

Tom McManus.

Kilmarnock helped the club reach the 2001 Scottish Cup final and he could consider himself unlucky to be omitted from the squad that day. As it was, he won several Under-21 caps before settling into first-team duties.

However, Tam was rather unfortunate with injury and sustained a broken ankle against Dundee in January 2002 that hampered his career. From making his debut in May 1999 at Stranraer to playing a key role in the 2002/03 campaign, he had to endure the rough and the smooth that football can throw up.

A useful goalscorer, he could strike from distance and hit memorable counters in defeats at Celtic and Rangers – both of which were contenders for goal of the season.

He moved to Boston United on loan in August 2004 shortly after Tony Mowbray took command of the side, but it was hardly an easy ride and he returned homesick. Alas, by that time he was well down the strikers' pecking order and a move to Dundee in January 2005 ended his lengthy association with Hibs.
Appearances: 107 Goals: 18

McNAMARA Jackie

Jackie was suffering dreadfully with his knees at Celtic when Eddie Turnbull offered him the chance to come to Hibs in 1977. Hibs physio John McNiven suggested that twenty-four-year-old Jackie could recover and McNiven's expertise was vital, because within months of arriving McNamara had to undergo a cartilage operation.

In signing for Hibs what Jackie never knew throughout the negotiations was that the legendary Pat Stanton would be going in the other direction. So he arrived at Easter Road, to be greeted with simmering resentment. However, McNamara had nine years at Hibs and received a testimonial against Newcastle United.

There were many highs to his career at Easter Road, including the 1979 Scottish Cup final run that saw Hibs beat Aberdeen and

Jackie McNamara.

Hearts en route to a twice replayed final with Rangers. The low point was being relegated in 1980.

Not noted for his goalscoring, he got his first against Leicester City in a friendly in the Midlands and then went 64 games before popping up with a cracker in a cup-tie at Rangers.

John Blackley freed McNamara when his knees were pretty well 'gone' and John McNiven had done all he could. Allan McGraw had just been made Morton manager and convinced McNamara that he could continue at a less demanding level. Little did Jackie know that a wonderful swansong was about to happen. McNamara, who had always hated playing at Greenock, joined when the 'Ton were bottom of the First Division but helped them embark on a 17-match unbeaten run.

His son played with Dunfermline before moving successfully to Celtic and earning Scotland caps.
Appearances: 236 Goals: 2

McNAMEE John

Arguably, in the modern game John would have experienced problems with referees. His philosophy, at least from the touchline view, appeared to be to make the opposition strikers aware of his presence. An early robust tackle was a popular approach.

A huge centre half, John was Jock Stein's first major Hibernian signing, coming to the club from Celtic in April 1964. In short he was an uncompromising player who could frighten his own players as much as the opposition. Pat Stanton tells a lovely story of how John would turn to the Hibs players before a match and state baldly: 'Any of yous goes hidin' today an' you'll have me to answer to.' Given John's size and notorious temper it was advice that was more often heeded than not!

He arrived at Easter Road with quite a reputation. His vendetta with Celtic teammate John Hughes was a quirky but hugely entertaining

John McNamee.

sideshow during his spell with Celtic. Respected football writer Glenn Gibbons tells a wonderful story of how Hughes, a considerable success, was one of the first players at Celtic to own a car. He would drive past McNamee, who would be standing at a bus stop on his way to Parkhead. This fuelled the animosity that existed and which would spill out at training, where Hughes and McNamee would go at each other with gusto.

Hibs fans welcomed their new centre half. He did not let them down – well, not often – but he was sent off against Celtic in the 1965 League Cup semi-final replay at Ibrox. A veritable man-mountain, he was as uncompromising as he was fearsome. He served Hibs from 1964 to December 1966, when he moved on to Newcastle United.

John played over 100 League games for Newcastle before squeezing in spells with Blackburn, Hartlepool, Lancaster City and Morton.

Appearances: 77 Goals: 4

McNEIL George

Arguably better known as a sprinter, McNeil joined Hibs in the mid-1960s. An apprentice quantity surveyor, he had shown athletic prowess at Ross High School in Tranent and by the time he was with Hibs he was competing in the prestigious Powderhall New Year's Day Sprint.

Appearances: 1 Goals: 0

McNEIL Matt

A 6ft 2in centre half, Matt joined Hibernian from Ashfield Juniors with high hopes but was unable to move beyond being a fringe player at Easter Road. He played in the League Cup clash with Falkirk in August 1949 and managed only one League outing that term before seeking pastures new.

He was sold to Newcastle United in December 1949 for a fee of £10,000. Later he played with Barnsley, Brighton and Norwich.

Born in Glasgow in July 1927, his only problem at Easter Road was clearly the level of competition in what was a championship-winning side.

Appearances: 1 Goals: 0

McQUEEN Tommy

Tommy went from Burnbank Athletic to Motherwell when he was only sixteen but he failed to make the grade at Fir Park and moved to Leith Athletic. He then reverted to junior football with Kilbirnie Ladeside, where he won a junior cup badge.

He made his Hibernian debut in a friendly against Bolton Wanderers in April 1952 and went on to register three League outings during that season. Unable to secure a regular slot in the first team, he moved to Dunfermline Athletic in the summer of 1953.

Appearances: 3 Goals: 0

McQUILKEN Jamie

Joined Hibs in December 1996 having served an apprenticeship at Celtic before moving on to Dundee United. His debut came in a 1–4 reversal to Celtic. Jamie, who had two Scotland Under-21 caps, failed to settle at Easter Road and made only 10 League outings as a Hibee.

Appearances: 10 Goals: 0

McWILLIAMS Derek

Pitched into the Hibernian side as a raw sixteen-year-old in 1982, he showed enough in his early games (both against Clydebank) to suggest a decent career could lie ahead.

However, that career was to be spent largely away from Easter Road. More readily associated with Falkirk, Partick Thistle and Dunfermline, Derek was a strong-running midfielder with a degree of 'bite' to his game.

Appearances: 2 Goals: 0

McWILLIAMS Walter

Played just two League games for Hibs but scored once, so could be reasonably happy with his contribution. Both of his matches for Hibs came in the 1956/57 season. He moved to Cowdenbeath in May 1957

Appearances: 2 Goals: 1

MILLEN Andy

Born in Kilmarnock in 1965, Andy played for Alloa, Hamilton, St Johnstone and Killie before joining Hibs in March 1995. He came to Easter Road in a deal that took Billy Findlay to Kilmarnock in exchange.

He was a fringe player with Hibs but, considering he had only turned full-time with St Johnstone, made up for lost time rapidly. Andy won a 'B' international cap for Scotland against Wales and picked up two B&Q Cup winner's badges from his time at Hamilton.

After leaving Hibs in January 1997 he played with Raith Rovers, Ayr United, Morton and Clyde.

Appearances: 52 Goals: 0

MILLER Graeme

Born in 1973, Graeme joined Hibs straight from school. He played outside left and was part of the Miller dynasty at Easter Road – his father Alex managed the club at one point and younger brother Greg was also on the playing staff.

Appearances: 3 Goals: 0

MILLER Greg

Unable to make the expected impact at Easter Road, Greg moved to Motherwell and then on to Clydebank. With the Bankies in deep financial trouble, he was forced to move on again and joined Swedish Second Division side Vasteras. He returned to Scotland to join Brechin City in January 2000.

Appearances: 12 Goals: 1

MILLER Kenny

Quick and agile, Kenny joined Hibs in 1996 from Hutcheson Vale BC. Arguably it was a spell spent on loan to Stenhousemuir though that really ignited his career. He scored twice on his debut for the Warriors and returned to Hibs a more confident player. Soon the goals came and when he popped in counters against Hearts, Celtic and Rangers it was clear he was a confident young striker who could go far in the game.

Alas, just as he was hammering on the door of a Scotland call-up (having achieved Under-21 status), Rangers bought him for £2 million. His departure created much anguish among a Hibernian support – which felt it had a new Baker or Reilly in its midst.

He started sensationally at Ibrox, even scoring five in one SPL match against St Mirren, but he soon fell from the picture. He was eventually sold to Wolves just days after Alex McLeish took over as Rangers boss. With Wolves he won promotion to the FA Premiership and enjoyed national headlines when scoring a fabulous winner against the mighty Manchester United in 2004.

Had Kenny stayed with Hibernian who knows what might have transpired?
Appearances: 45 Goals: 13

MILLER Willie (1)

A talented goalkeeper, Willie had played for Celtic and Scotland when he joined Hibs in January 1954 from Clyde. In truth, manager Hugh Shaw had signed Willie as cover for Hamilton and Younger and the Glaswegian, who was a qualified locomotive engineer, spent much of his time looking after his 'Miller's Bar' in Townhead, Glasgow.
Appearances: 3 Goals: 0

MILLER Willie (2)

A fiercely competitive full-back, Willie was signed from Edina Hibs in 1987, and made his

Willie Miller.

debut in February 1990 against Celtic. He made swift progress thereafter and was capped seven times by Scotland at Under-21 level. He proved popular with the Hibernian support – largely by dint of his physical approach to the game and whole-hearted commitment.

Between 1989 and 1998 he made an excellent 246 appearances, of which seven were as a substitute. The highlight of his time at Easter Road was surely being part and parcel of the side that won the League Cup against Dunfermline in 1991.

From Easter Road, Willie moved to Dundee where he was a regular for a few seasons until joining Keith Wright at Cowdenbeath.
Appearances: 246 Goals: 1

MILNE Arthur

In 1934 Arthur moved from Brechin Vics to Dundee United and thus began a most interesting career. A prolific marksman he moved to Liverpool in March 1937 on loan but was not returned to Dundee United. He joined

Willie McCartney's Hibernian and in June 1941 scored within 20 seconds of the start of a famous 5–2 Hibs win at Celtic (indeed, he bagged a hat-trick that day). Alas, his career was nearing an end when football resumed after the Second World War. He did play in three matches in the 1946/47 season and netted a single goal at the expense of Kilmarnock in a 6–0 win.
Appearances: 3 Goals: 1

MILNE Calumn

Calumn was only seventeen when Hibs signed him from Salveson Boys Club in April 1983. He never quite settled into the team and after eight seasons at the club had only just made the 50 appearances mark.

His career was clearly hampered by injury and – perhaps less so – by indiscipline. He was sent off against Rangers in 1991 – a dismissal that infuriated Hibs boss Alex Miller.
Appearances: 79 Goals: 0

MITCHELL Graham

Born in Glasgow in 1962, Graham joined Hamilton Accies from Auchengill BC in 1979. He became one of their finest defenders and stayed with them until late December 1986, when he joined Hibs.

He soon forged a strong defensive partnership with Gordon Rae and this would continue when Gordon Hunter moved into central defence. He won a League Cup winner's badge in 1991 and was in the side beaten by Rangers at Celtic Park in the same tournament two years later. After a long and distinguished career with Hibs he was freed in May 1996 and made the short journey to Falkirk.
Appearances: 265 Goals: 3

MORAN Dougie

A talented youngster at Hibernian, Dougie suffered from a lack of first-team opportunities and elected to try his luck away from

Graham Mitchell.

Easter Road. He made a very good job of it too.

In 1953/54 he made the ideal start to his Hibs career. Playing one League game he made it a scoring debut, netting the winner in a 2–1 victory over St Mirren.

He went to Falkirk in January 1957 and quickly helped them win the Scottish Cup (a trophy that had eluded Hibs since 1902). Then, in July 1961, he moved on to Ipswich Town where he was an integral part of their finest team in years. He returned to Scotland with Dundee United but could not settle and joined Falkirk once more.
Appearances: 3 Goals: 1

MORROW Sam

Sam made his Hibernian debut as a playing substitute in Hibs' weather-stricken first leg

Intertoto match against FK Vetra at Easter Road. Tall and quick, Tony Mowbray had signed him in July 2004, largely on the strength of their having worked together at Ipswich Town.

Sam had joined Ipswich when he was fifteen but found first-team openings limited. In December 2003 he went to Boston United for a month on loan. A former Northern Ireland Under-19 international, he initially found himself in a queue for a forward's spot behind Riordan, O'Connor, McManus, Dobbie and Shiels.

MUIR George

A left-back, he came to Hibernian in 1955 from the then prolific nursery of Edinburgh Thistle. George made 24 appearances in 1956/57 and in the words of Lawrie Reilly 'had a very good left foot'.

In later life he worked on the tollbooths on the Forth Road Bridge.
Appearances: 49 Goals: 0

MUIR Lindsay

Signed as a schoolboy, Lindsay was an international at that level and he came into the first team in 1976 after starring in the pre-season tour of Ireland. Strong and determined, he was an attacking midfielder. Yet for all his promise he failed to make an impression.

In 1978 he joined St Johnstone and he stayed there for two seasons before moving south to Berwick Rangers.
Appearances: 18 Goals: 1

MUIRHEAD Billy

Raised in Musselburgh, Billy was a goalkeeper who had a brief flirtation with first-team football in season 1959/60. He played in 15 matches that campaign and in half a dozen the next. But the arrival of Ronnie Simpson finally killed off his Hibernian career. He later

played in Toronto and then arguably less glamorous surroundings at Raith Rovers.
Appearances: 21 Goals: 0

MULKERRIN Jim

A centre forward, he joined Hibs in 1950 from Dumbarton Strollers. At only 5ft 6in he had to have that little extra to succeed in that position.

He played a couple of games in the 1951 Championship team but sought success elsewhere and signed for Accrington Stanley in March 1957. It was a move that worked well and he scored a very impressive 36 goals in 70 matches. Later in his career he played for Tranmere.
Appearances: 16 Goals: 8

MUNRO Iain

A refined and cultured player, Iain Munro was a delight to watch. His cerebral approach and almost artistic use of the ball, allied to a wonderfully balanced athleticism, made him a tremendous team player. There was a considerable gnashing of teeth when he left Hibs for Rangers in 1976, a feeling which lingered when the players received in exchange – Ally Scott and Graham Fyfe – failed to live up to expectations.

Ian had joined St Mirren in 1968 but was farmed out to Cambuslang Rangers and Blantyre Vics before joining full time in 1969. A physical education teacher by trade, he was part-time at St Mirren until Hibs signed him in 1972 and he played in the 1973 Dryburgh Cup final win over Celtic and in the 1974 League Cup final against the same opponents.

His move to Rangers did not really work out and he returned to St Mirren before joining Stoke City, Sunderland and Dundee United. John Blackley convinced Iain to rejoin Hibs and he enjoyed a fine twilight to his career, playing in another League Cup final and a Scottish Cup semi-final.

Retiring at thirty-five, he then entered coaching and managed Dunfermline, Dundee, Hamilton Accies and Raith Rovers.
Appearances: 94 Goals: 11

MUNRO John

In the 1950/51 League season Hibernian used twenty-three players and right-winger John Munro was one of them, making a single outing. He had been signed from Bathgate Thistle and had – rather unfortunately and unfairly – been labelled 'the new Gordon Smith'.
Appearances: 1 Goals: 0

MURDOCK Colin

A full Northern Ireland international, Colin joined Hibernian in July 2003. He started his senior career at Manchester United and was a contemporary in the United youth side of players such as Beckham and Giggs. He moved to Preston North End and made over 100 outings for the Deepdale club before joining Hibs.

Initially viewed with scepticism and indeed downright hostility by some sections of the Hibs support, he had to work hard to win the doubters over. Gradually his dominance in the air and sheer guts won the fans over – that and the flawless conversion of the decisive penalty in the 2003 CIS Cup semi-final win over Rangers!
Appearances: 32 Goals: 3

MURPHY David

Signed by Tony Mowbray in the summer of 2004, David was a former England Youth cap who had found first-team openings limited at multi-international Middlesbrough. A delightfully energetic left wing-back, he was soon making an impression at Hibs, particularly when scoring in a 2–2 draw at home to Celtic.

MURPHY John

A talented Hibs youngster under Bob Shankly, John made fleeting first-team appearances and played on the tour of Nigeria. In June 1971 he left Hibs to join Morton, but after 70 games for the Greenock club he was on his travels once more, this time Stirling Albion being the destination. He brought the curtain down on his senior career with a spell at Cowdenbeath.
Appearances: 8 Goals: 1

MURRAY Gary

Born in Dundee in 1959, he had shone for Montrose against Hibs in a 1979 League Cup tie and a note was made of his name. This was duly followed up and he joined Hibs in December 1980 for £60,000.

One of Gary's great strengths was that he could play wide on the left as well as straight down the centre. Strong in the air, he was also adept at cutting in from wide positions and using his shooting power to good effect.

He made his debut for Hibs in the First Division against Stirling Albion and had his first goal a few weeks later in a 1–0 win over Dumbarton. Gary Murray served Hibs from 1980 to 1984, starring in 79 League matches and grabbing 16 goals in that time.

He moved to Forfar in 1984 and two years later was back at Montrose. He helped the club win promotion to the First Division and in all scored 91 goals for the Gable Endies.
Appearances: 79 Goals: 16

MURRAY Ian

A product of the Hibernian youth system, Ian Murray epitomised all that was good in a young player. He was full of enthusiasm, dedicated to learning and had the additional bonus of being a big Hibernian supporter.

He quickly progressed from being a fringe player at Easter Road to being a key member

Ian Murray.

of Scotland's Under-21 side and, rather fittingly, won his first full Scotland cap at Easter Road in 2002 (against Canada and in opposition to teammate Paul Fenwick). By that time he had played in a Scottish Cup final and briefly captained Hibs.

He joined Hibernian from Dundee United and made his debut against that club in January 1999. His first goal came in a Scottish Cup tie against Dunfermline and by 2002/03 he was leading the Hibernian goalscoring charts – from midfield!

One of Ian's key qualities was being able to raise his game in crunch matches and he scored a valuable goal against St Johnstone when Hibs faced relegation and had appointed Bobby Williamson as boss. He adamantly believed that he had benefited enormously from a loan spell at Alloa in January 2001 during the Alex McLeish era.

He earned a degree of notoriety in some parts for having the date 1973 dyed into his hair prior to the winter 2002 derby clash at Tynecastle.

Appearances: 112 Goals: 12

Willie Murray.

N

MURRAY Willie

A speedy forward, Willie was a fringe player in the Turnbull's Tornadoes years. He could take a chance when presented, however, and was the kind of busy player that supporters could relate to.

Born in Edinburgh in 1954, he joined Hibs in October 1970. Although a member of the Scotland Youth team, patience was required on Willie's part before making his Hibernian breakthrough – he did not make his first-team debut until July 1972 against Waterford. Between 1973 and 1981 Willie played 77 League games for Hibs, 14 of them as a substitute.

Appearances: 77 Goals: 7

NELSON Dennis

Made just one appearance for Hibs, in the 1971/72 season, which was scant reward for this powerful little centre forward. There is no doubt that a broken leg, which he suffered early in his Hibs career, did his Easter Road prospects great harm.

Better times lay in store when he went to Dunfermline, Crewe, Reading and back to Crewe – where he was always a regular.

Appearances: 1 Goals: 0

NICHOLLS Dave

From Chelsea BC to Ferguslie United and then on to Hibernian was the early career route of this solid midfielder. He joined Hibs in 1989 but never quite held down a permanent first-team position and eventually moved to Coleraine in Northern Ireland.

From Ireland he returned to Scotland in 1994 to join Hamilton. Failure to establish himself there saw a move to Southern Ireland and Cork before Clydebank snapped him up. At this stage his promise began to mature and by the time he joined Falkirk he was a very competent midfielder indeed.

Appearances: 6 Goals: 0

NICOL Kevin

Kevin was signed by Franck Sauzee near the end of the Frenchman's brief reign in charge. A clever young midfielder, he was signed from Raith Rovers and took over from Grant Brebner when the latter was seriously injured in the Hibs-Rangers Scottish Cup tie of 2004. Kevin had three Scotland Under-19 caps to his name when he joined Hibs and was a noted devotee of the club gym when not playing. Alas, a couple of broken foot bones ruined his hopes in the 2004/05 season.

Appearances: 18 Goals: 1

NICOL Robert

In 1952 Hibs went to Edinburgh City to secure the services of centre half Robert Nicol. He found it hard to break into the Hibernian first team but grabbed a goal and 20 league appearances in 1956/57. He was capped against England at Under-23 level on two separate occasions.

Robert Benjamin Mathieson Nicol then moved to Barnsley before returning to Scotland with Berwick.

Appearances: 37 Goals: 2

NUTLEY Robert

This was another player whose best years were lost to the Second World War. Bobby was born in Paisley in September 1916 and only played in a single match for Hibs in the 1946/47 season before moving to Portsmouth in August 1946. He was thirty by the time he joined Pompey and only

managed nine matches for them before bringing the curtain down on his career at Queen of the South.

Appearances: 1 Goals: 0

O

O'BRIEN Gerry

Eddie Turnbull went to Clydebank in May 1978 to secure the services of Gerry and he quickly scored the winner in an East of Scotland Shield final to win over the supporters.

Born in Glasgow in 1949, he had previously played with Clydebank, Southampton, Bristol Rovers and Swindon.

Appearances: 7 Goals: 0

O'CONNOR Garry

A glut of goals in the Hibernian Under-18 and Under-21 sides catapulted young Garry straight into the Hibernian first team in 2000. He responded with all four goals in a 4–0 pre-season win at Gala Fairydean.

A powerful young striker, he was soon among the headlines; his first competitive strike came in a 1–1 draw against Celtic in February 2002. Thereafter he was a frequent scorer. So much so that he was capped by Scotland at full international level before making any appearances at Under-21 or lesser ranks. There was a precedent here as he had been voted Scotland's Player of the Year in April 2002, without having ever won the young version of this award.

Some of his goals were stuff of local legend. He hit a belter in a 3–0 win at Partick and scored the famous ninetieth minute winner against Hearts at Easter Road when Hibs won with only ten men in 2003.

Appearances: 76 Goals: 21

Garry O'Connor.

John O'Neil.

O'NEIL John

A clever and creative midfielder, John O'Neil was signed by Alex McLeish in the summer of 2000. He was the fifth signing of a busy period and was seen by many as a direct replacement for the departing Pat McGinlay. A Bosman signing from St Johnstone, he quickly settled into the Hibs side and for three years was a key element in the teams of McLeish, Sauzee and Williamson.

Sadly, an injury sustained in the first derby fixture of the 2002/03 season ruled him out for the opening three months of the campaign; when he returned to full fitness he failed to impose himself in quite the same manner. Thus, by May 2003, he had been told that at the age of thirty-one he was able to leave.

John had several highlights in his time at Easter Road. He was a key player in the side that reached the 2001 Scottish Cup final – indeed, he scored the opening goal in the semi-final against Livingston at Hampden. His form was such that he was also capped by Scotland that year (against Poland) but Hibs fans will no doubt think the highlight was his sensational goal for Hibs in the 6–2 win over Hearts at Easter Road. A rising shot from the edge of the box, the goal gave Hibs a 5–1 lead and was evidence that it was going to be a night to remember.

Prior to playing with Hibs he had been with Dundee United and St Johnstone, and upon leaving Easter Road he joined Falkirk.
Appearances: 86 Goals: 10

O'NEILL Michael

Michael spent three seasons with Hibernian and impressed as a speedy and thoughtful

123

Michael O'Neill.

player, in the mould of an old-fashioned inside forward. One of his key strengths was his eye for goal and his tally while at Easter Road was impressive.

Capped 34 times by Northern Ireland (he was born in Portadown), Michael had a nomadic career that was sadly blighted by injury, particularly a major groin problem that necessitated five operations. He started his career with Coleraine in Northern Ireland then joined Newcastle United (where he was a teammate of Paul Gascoigne) before serving Coventry, Dundee United, Hibernian, Aberdeen, Reading, Wigan, Portland Timbers, St Johnstone and Clydebank.

He had a sharp temper and quick tongue and this contributed to his sending off in the Edinburgh derby of January 1995. But the overall impression left is of a quicksilver forward who scored regularly.

Appearances: 98 Goals: 19

OGILVIE John

Signed from Thorniewood United in 1946, Ogilvie broke into the Hibs team as a left-half but had more luck at left-back. He played in 35 matches and was cruelly denied the chance to exploit his talents by injury.

He helped Hibs overcome Aberdeen in a twice-replayed League Cup quarter-final, but could not stop Motherwell beating Hibs 3–0 in the final at Hampden.

Motherwell was to prove the dreaded name in the Ogilvie career. In the 1951 Scottish Cup semi-final at Tynecastle against 'The Steelmen' John suffered a transverse fraction. This bad leg break set him back and it is doubtful that he was ever the same player again. Given that he was a native of Motherwell (and had to swim at Motherwell baths to recuperate) this was a doubly ironic blow.

He missed the entire 1951/52 and 1952/53 seasons and managed just one match in the 1953/54 campaign, so the severity of his injury is easy to gauge.

Eventually he moved to Leicester City and he served them from 1955 to 1958. Thereafter there was a short spell at Mansfield before he settled to life in Leicester.

Appearances: 35 Goals: 0

ORMAN Alen

A Bosnian by birth, Alen and his family moved to Austria when civil war erupted in what was then Yugoslavia. He made football his career and earned a contract with Admira Wacker in Vienna. His displays there were sufficiently good to interest Belgian side Royal Antwerp.

He joined Hibernian in the summer of 2001 and looked to be a pacy overlapping full-back. His stock on the terraces at Easter Road rose considerably when he scored a screamer at Ibrox Park in a 2–2 draw. Never spectacular, he was however extremely industrious and showed pace when going forward – so much so that he became the first Hibs player to be capped by Austria when he played against Norway in late 2002.

A dramatic end to the year followed with Alen suffering an epileptic fit in a match against Rangers, but he quickly recovered and was none the worse for his experience. Never picked that frequently under Bobby Williamson, he did better under Tony Mowbray and rediscovered his scoring touch in late 2004.

Appearances: 73 Goals: 2

ORMOND Willie

Signed from Stenhousemuir in November 1946, William Esplin Ormond was unique in that he was the only member of the Famous Five who cost Hibs a transfer fee, albeit a minimal £1,200. A traditional outside left, he stayed for fifteen years and throughout that time proved himself an expert chance maker and goal-taker.

Willie Ormond pictured with his two brothers from Airdrie.

Sadly, his Hibs career was dogged by injury and after breaking his leg against Aberdeen in a cup tie he went on to break it twice more and also suffered ruptured ligaments in a Scottish Cup tie against Motherwell. To cap things off he also suffered a broken arm. Nevertheless, despite these multiple injury setbacks, he continued to bounce back and, like all the other members of the Famous Five, was to top the 100 goals mark in his Hibernian career.

Equally impressive was his ability to forge a Scotland career. He had picked up seven Scottish League caps before the international selectors picked him for the full team. But there was a strange shape to his Scotland appearances as he picked up five caps in

1954 and then had to wait patiently until completing his six-cap collection in 1959 against England.

Like his fellow Famous Five teammates the only significant honour to elude Willie was a Scottish Cup winner's badge. The nearest he came to touching the silverware was in 1958 when Hibs went down to Clyde 1–0, and there was an acceptance among many after that game that the Famous Five had never been destined to taste cup glory. Willie had played in the 1947 final against Aberdeen as well.

It was often said that Willie's strength lay in his pace and his directness, but clearly there must have been more to him than that to explain such a long career. He proved as useful to Hibs as a veteran as he had a youngster and stayed at Easter Road until the summer of 1961 when he moved to Falkirk.

Eventually he became assistant trainer at Brockville and began a move into football coaching that took him to the very pinnacle of the Scottish game in January 1973 – when he was appointed Scotland manager. The fact that ensured he would become Scotland supremo was surely his magnificent spell as St Johnstone manager. He moulded the Perth side into an exciting outfit that waded into Europe with style and regularly pushed near the top of the table.

Scotland performed well in the 1974 World Cup finals in Germany, returning home unbeaten, and Ormond was rewarded with an OBE twelve months later. His love of Edinburgh, however, was never far from the surface and in May 1977 he became Hearts' boss. Sadly, that did not work out the way he had hoped and in January 1980 he moved out of Tynecastle. Naturally enough his next port of call was Easter Road, where he worked with Eddie Turnbull briefly, before taking over in March 1980. Alas, poor health had begun to take its toll and his stay in the Hibs hot seat was short lived.

Willie died in May 1984 and was mourned throughout the Scottish game; such was the high esteem with which this highly likeable man was held. To this day, his record in the World Cup as Scotland manager remains unsurpassed.

Appearances: 348 Goals: 133

O'ROURKE Jimmy

One of the most popular Hibernian players of the Eddie Turnbull management era, it is often overlooked that Jim O'Rourke was with Hibernian long before Eddie was appointed boss. Jim joined Hibernian in 1962 from schools football and stayed until 1974. His subsequent career took him to St Johnstone and then Motherwell before he returned to Easter Road as reserve team coach to Eddie Turnbull.

Brought up as a Hibernian supporter, he had watched the team from 1951 onwards. As he once confessed to me: 'Every game as a Hibernian player was a great occasion for me because for so long I had followed the club from the terraces'.

His debut came on 9 December 1962 and was against Utrecht of Holland in the Fairs Cup. Only sixteen at the time, manager Walter Galbraith shrewdly delayed telling Jim of his bow until the very afternoon of the match.

Quite simply, O'Rourke loved scoring goals and he had the good fortune to play in sides that provided him with plenty of opportunities. Playing up front with Alan Gordon was perhaps his zenith, but the partner he most enjoyed was Joe Baker – who had been a particular boyhood hero.

The highlight of O'Rourke's time at Easter Road was never in any doubt. In an emotional interview Jim once told me: 'For me the highlight of my time at Easter Road was the 1972 League Cup final when we finally got our hands on the silverware we thoroughly deserved. It was such an important win for the players and for their families. Coming from a Hibs family it provided a wonderful sense of achievement.'

December 1972 and January 1973 were the halcyon days for Hibernian fans, when the team truly delivered the supporters to the football equivalent of the Promised Land. On 9 December Hibs defeated Celtic 2–1 in the League Cup final and then, on the following Saturday, not only was the cup paraded around Easter Road but Hibs crushed Ayr United 8–1. With a goal in the final, a hat-trick against Ayr and then a brace in the January 1973 massacre of Hearts at Tynecastle (when 7–0 was scant reward for the most one-sided derby in history) the part played by O'Rourke could never be overplayed.

Jim O'Rourke.

Jim left for St Johnstone in 1974, where ex-Hibs coach John Lambie was on the staff, and with a wonderful sense of irony his first goal for the Saints came in a 1–0 win over Hibernian at Easter Road on 28 September 1974.

Appearances: 210 Goals: 81

ORR Neil

Neil's father, Tommy, had been a respected international with Morton and Neil was a chip off the old block. He played over 200 games for Morton (League Cup and Scottish Cup semi-finals included) before earning a big money move to West Ham in December 1981 (the fee was said to total £300,000). He spent just over five seasons in London before Hibs came calling with a £100,000 cheque.

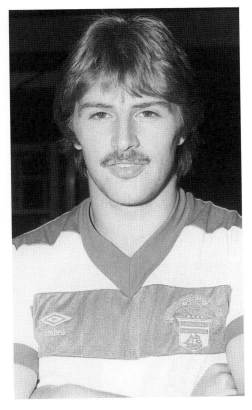

Neil Orr.

His debut came against Queen of the South at Easter Road and Neil scored in a 3–1 win. He was also one of Hibernian's scorers against Morton on the day that goalkeeper Andy Goram scored with a downfield punt.

After a useful spell with Hibernian Neil joined St Mirren.

Appearances: 166 Goals: 3

P

PAATELAINEN Mixu

A Finnish international, Mixu joined Hibernian in 1998 from Wolverhampton Wanderers and proved a most astute purchase. His goals not only helped Hibs escape from the First Division but, once back in the Premier League, he showed enough experience and goal awareness to be a major player. He famously scored three times against Hearts in a 6–2 win at Easter Road in October 2000.

Mixu came to Scotland with Dundee United in 1987 from Valkeakosken Haka. In total he scored 33 goals for Dundee United and this earned him moves to Aberdeen, Bolton and then Wolves.

What Paatelainen gave Hibernian was a tremendous target man who was both capable of scoring himself or producing the killer knockdown for his colleagues. He led the line with immense muscle and was a wonderful escape route if the Hibs defence was under pressure. Quite simply, they had only to knock the ball up to Mixu to gather some valuable breathing space.

In the summer of 2001 he moved from Edinburgh to Strasbourg in France but spent an unhappy season there, playing only eight matches. He rejoined Hibernian shortly into the 2002/03 campaign and had his first goal in the awful 4–1 home defeat by Dunfermline. However, things picked up following that reverse and he led the line with his usual mix of enthusiasm and knowhow as the season wore on.

While we can recall plenty of great goals by Mixu, it has to be said he will also be 'fondly' remembered for a quite stunning last minute penalty miss against Hearts in 2001. The award was controversial to begin with but when Mixu ran up and halted at the last second he completely foxed his Finnish colleague Anti Niemi in the Hearts goal. Alas, the chip that Mixu then executed was a shade too high and the ball clipped the crossbar on its way over an empty net!

Mixu scored 18 goals in gaining 70 full Finland international caps but he retired fairly early from the national scene, preferring to preserve his energies for club football after what was by any standards a lengthy international career.

Equally impressive was Mixu's demeanour off the park. He made enormous time to talk to fans, sign autographs and generally make himself available. Unfailingly polite would be my description of Mixu, and to interview him was always a genuine pleasure.
Appearances: 117 Goals: 38

PARKE John

A talented full-back, John, who was born in Belfast in 1937, was signed from Linfield in October 1963. Although he played in only 21 League games for Hibs it was clear that he was a very talented individual indeed and with every performance he seemed to improve.

It was always going to be a battle hanging on to such a prodigious talent and he was sold to high-spending Sunderland in November 1964. He settled well on Wearside and played in a century of games for Sunderland. One of his claims to fame while at Roker Park was playing in the 0–5 defeat to Manchester United when David Herd scored a hat-trick with each goal against a different

Sunderland goalkeeper (injuries having forced changes).

John won 14 caps for Northern Ireland and moved from Sunderland to Belgian football.
Appearances: 21 Goals: 0

PATERSON Craig

The son of John Paterson, Craig quickly proved himself to be an outstanding prospect at centre half and, while commanding in the air and solid on the ground, he also displayed a neat use of the ball.

Craig was signed in December 1977 and made his debut against Dundee in a friendly fixture at Dens Park in February 1978, although his League bow did not come until August 1979. Thereafter he edged his way increasingly into the first-team picture.

Capped by Scotland at Under-21 level, he was a rock at the heart of the Hibs defence in the early 1980s and was voted Hibernian

Craig Paterson.

Jock Paterson, third from right in the back row.

Player of the Year in 1981. Sadly he left for Rangers in July 1982 for a fee in the region of £225,000. It was money that cash-strapped Hibs could hardly refuse and at the time it represented a record fee for the Glasgow club.

He won a League Cup winner's badge at Rangers, a Scottish Cup medal at Motherwell and then finished his top rate career at Kilmarnock.

He squeezed in spells with Hamilton, Glenafton and Forth Wanderers before settling on a career in the media as a radio pundit. In his role as Radio Forth match summariser, I would bump into Craig in many of the pressrooms up and down Scotland and he always had a cheery word. His tales of his career were enormously entertaining.

One regret I have, however, concerns a dark evening in the car park behind Easter Road. My car would not start and Craig rather suspected it was a flat battery but the noise when I tried to turn the engine over was most unusual and he put away his jump leads and suggested I call the rescue service. Thus shivering to the bone I waved goodnight to Craig. Over an hour later the roadside assistance arrived and the mechanic said: 'Ah, a flat battery. I'll have you up and running in no time.' Given that it was the coldest night of the year, how I wish Craig's mechanical knowledge had matched his football know-how!
Appearances: 104 Goals: 4

PATERSON Jock

Born in Colchester, England, 'Jock' worked as a representative for a brewery firm and was a versatile defender, capable of playing either centre-back or left-back. Signed from Penicuik Thistle in 1944, he was capped by the Scottish League against Wales in 1953.

Playing first-team football from 1948 through to 1960, there is little doubt that Jock was one of the great Hibernian servants.

He was an ever present in the 1951 and 1952 championship-winning sides and in all played in a staggering 283 league games for Hibs.

There was a degree of stability in the Hibs defence at this time and Paterson's fitness served him well. He did not venture into the opposition half too often hence the distinction he has of being the outfield player to have played the most games in Hibs colours without scoring a single goal.

He spent a couple of seasons with Ayr in the early sixties but it is as a Hibee that he will always be remembered.
Appearances: 283 Goals: 0

PATERSON Willie

Signed in 1975 as a teenager, Willie had been with Burnley for two seasons before becoming home sick. He made his debut at Motherwell late in the 1975/76 season, earning a penalty within minutes of coming on as a substitute.

Early in the 1976/77 season Willie had the pleasure of scoring the Hibs goal in the October Edinburgh derby that ended 1–1. The Kilsyth-based winger moved to Falkirk in 1979 having made 11 outings as a Hibee.
Appearances: 11 Goals: 2

PATON Eric

A short and stocky youngster who could not quite impose himself on the Hibernian scene during Alex McLeish's years, he later played for Partick Thistle, Morton and Queen of the South.
Appearances: 4 Goals: 0

PEAT Willie

A very versatile left-sided player Willie scored three goals from 11 outings in the 1946/47 season. However, he hankered for more regular first-team football and elected to try his luck elsewhere.

He moved to St Johnstone in 1947 and played over 100 games for the Perth outfit between 1947 and 1952.
Appearances: 11 Goals: 4

PETERS Allan

Registered with Hibernian on 20 September 1985 Allan had been signed from Tynecastle Boys Club. A substitute outing in the 1986/87 season was the only match in which he featured.
Appearances: 1 Goals: 0

PLENDERLEITH John

A joiner by trade, Jackie (as he was known) was signed in 1954 from Armadale Thistle. He was a Scottish Youth international and became a Hibs regular shortly after his eighteenth

John Plenderleith.

birthday. His debut came in the 1954/55 season and over the next couple of seasons he impressed sufficiently to earn three Under-23 caps for Scotland.

In July 1960 he moved to Manchester City and he spent two seasons at Maine Road. John won one full Scotland cap and five Under-23 caps in total.

Appearances: 123 Goals: 0

PLUMB Angus

This delightfully named forward joined Hibernian in 1948 from Armadale Thistle. Manager Hugh Shaw could be well pleased with his signing for early in 1949 he scored in five consecutive League games.

Sadly competition was fierce at Easter Road and with Smith, Linwood, Cuthbertson and Reilly all pushing for places Angus was sold to Falkirk in December 1949.

He did not forgive Hibs easily and scored within 30 seconds in a thrilling 5–4 Hibs League Cup win (Hibs went on to reach the final against Motherwell in that season). He still delighted Hibs fans from time to time, however, while at Falkirk… most notably by scoring three for the Bairns in a 5–4 win over Hearts in March 1951.

After Falkirk he played with East Fife but the feeling is that with seven goals from seven games in his first season at Easter Road he was extremely unlucky not to carve out a longer career with Hibs. Angus was English, having been born in Woolwich.

Appearances: 7 Goals: 7

POWER Lee

Joined Hibernian as a twenty-five-year-old from Dundee, along with Paul Tosh, in a £200,000 deal in March 1997, having previously spent his career in England. Born in Lewisham he had served Norwich, Charlton, Sunderland, Portsmouth, Bradford City, Millwall and Peterborough United. At 6ft tall

he should have been able to lift Jim Duffy's side but failed to have the expected impact. In all Lee played only 11 league games in the colours of Hibernian.

Appearances: 11 Goals: 2

PRENDERVILLE Barry

Joined Hibs in September 1998 on loan from Coventry City and proved a most able fullback. Born in Dublin in 1976 he would have been an ideal asset for Hibs full time but after his loan spell expired he was unable to come to a more permanent arrangement.

Barry played 13 League games in Hibernian's promotion-winning season of 1998/99 and scored goals against both Morton and St Mirren. He came back to Scotland to play with Ayr United at one stage, then served St Patrick's Athletic and Oldham Athletic.

Appearances: 13 Goals: 2

PRESTON Tommy

Born in Edinburgh, Tommy played with Juniper Thistle, Edinburgh Thistle and Newtongrange Star before becoming a Hibee in 1953. A very versatile player he could play any of the inside positions and at one point was a centre forward replacement for Lawrie Reilly.

Signed by Hugh Shaw, Tommy was given his first-team debut in 1954 against Celtic. He played three matches at the tail end of the 1953/54 season and by his own admission was greatly reliant upon the advice of Sammy Kean during his early days at Easter Road.

At the end of that first season he toured Germany and Czechoslovakia with the club and stood in at centre forward for the ill Lawrie Reilly. The goals came easily and at the start of the 1954/55 season he was a prolific marksman before Lawrie returned to first-team duties.

Just how prolific he was is best gauged by the following statistics. He played in six

League Cup sectional ties and scored eight goals (amazingly that was not good enough to ensure that Hibs qualified for the quarter-final stages). He also scored our opening goal of the League campaign that term when we drew 1–1 at Rangers.

Tommy figured in some magnificent Hibernian matches. High in that list would be the epic Fairs Cup clashes with Barcelona, Tommy himself reckoning that the 4–4 draw Hibs achieved in the Nou Camp was even better than the 3–2 victory at Easter Road in the return leg. No recollection of Tommy could possibly be complete without reference to his four goals in an amazing 11–1 away win at Airdrie and he followed up with several goals in the 10–2 victory at Partick Thistle just weeks later.

The latter two games came in the 1959/60 season, which was a purple period for Tommy as he bagged 12 goals in only 17 matches.

A charming man to talk to, Tommy once told me that he was more famous in Edinburgh for his non-footballing activities. Sniffing the scent of scandal I asked him more but the explanation was quite innocent: 'An interesting thing that happened to me in my career was doing a bit of modelling. It was for the Ideal Homes Exhibition at Waverley Station and was during the close season. I used to joke that I earned more doing this than I did playing football! It meant my face became well known in Edinburgh because the show was featured regularly in *The Scotsman*.'

From Easter Road he moved to St Mirren but that did not last long and, with 228 League appearances for Hibs, it is understandable that he is forever associated with Hibernian.
Appearances: 228 Goals: 35

PRINGLE Alex

Signed in 1966 from Glasgow United, this Edinburgh born youngster was essentially a left half.

He made his first-team debut against St Johnstone in April 1969 and within a few years was helping the club in Scottish Cup semi-final ties and jousting with the best in Scotland.

His spell with Hibs was actually broken – he was granted a free transfer in 1970 and was set to emigrate to South Africa when Hibs changed their mind.

He later played with Dundee and Clyde as well as two North American sides.
Appearances: 8 Goals: 0

QUINN Pat

Prior to Mixu Paatelainen, Pat had the honour of being the last Hibernian player to score a hat-trick against Hearts. Signed in October 1963 from Blackpool, Pat was a clever, creative midfielder with a cultured left foot. He had made his name in Motherwell's talented Ancell Babes midfield, whom he joined in 1955 from Bridgeton Waverley.

While at Fir Park he was capped four times by Scotland, and six times by the Scottish League – making a rather unfortunate international debut in the 9–3 debacle against England at Wembley in 1961.

Pat joined Blackpool in 1962 but did not stay and a year later he joined Walter Galbraith's Hibernian side for £30,000. He settled quickly and had a goal at St Mirren just weeks later in a 1–1 draw. With his subtle promptings, several players thrived around him and Neil Martin went on to finish with 20 goals in his 28 League games that season. The following campaign (1964/65) Pat grabbed eight goals himself and was a part of the side that reached the Scottish Cup semi-final only to lose to Dunfermline at Tynecastle Park.

Pat Quinn.

After his Edinburgh playing days ended he moved to East Fife as player/assistant manager before taking up coaching roles with Partick Thistle, Hibs, Motherwell and Hamilton.
Appearances: 128 Goals: 19

R

RAE Gordon

The considerable frame and enormous heart of Gordon Rae served Hibs for thirteen seasons and whether he played as a centre forward or a centre half he proved extremely popular. He joined the club in 1975 from Whitehill Welfare and made his debut against Queen of the South in 1977. Three days later he scored in a 2–0 win at Rangers and his Hibs career was up and running.

Tall and strong, it was his determination that won Gordon a special place in the thoughts of Hibernian supporters. Over his long service he grew to personify Hibs and the supporters loved his never-say-die commitment. During his stint at Easter Road he won a First Division championship medal, played in the Scottish Cup final and sampled European nights. Among his many goals was one very important strike in a Scottish Cup quarter-final tie against Hearts at Easter Road in 1979. His was a career that basically covered the good and the bad times in Leith.

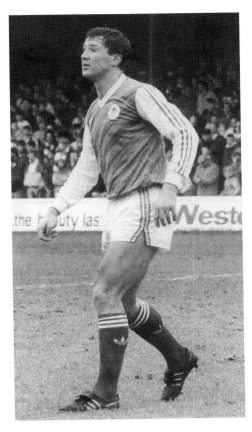

Gordon Rae.

When Gordon left it was to join Partick Thistle, for £65,000, where he won a promotion and made a favourable impression. Later he served Hamilton, Meadowbank, Gala, East Fife and Edinburgh City.

Appearances: 348 Goals: 47

RAE Robin

A goalkeeper, he made three outings in the 1981/82 season but was very much second fiddle, firstly to Jim McArthur, then Alan Rough.

He had joined Hibs from Musselburgh Windsor. From Easter Road he moved to Morton then Hamilton, but without conspicuous success at either. Remarkably he then dropped into junior football… as a striker, playing with Ormiston Primrose and Bonnyrigg Rose.

Appearances: 13 Goals: 0

RAYNES Steven

Scored in a pre-season friendly against Chelsea in August 1991. However, that super start was not built upon and he played only a handful of matches before disappearing from the Hibernian scene.

Appearances: 3 Goals: 0

REFVIK Isak

Although he played only a handful of games as a Hibernian player, the strange tale of Norwegian midfielder Isak Arne Refvik deserves to be placed on record.

Signed by Eddie Turnbull in the 1978/79 season, Refvik played five League games but really caught the eye in a League Cup tie against Morton in which he scored both Hibs goals in a 2–0 win. The win was all the more sweet as it came in a quarter-final tie where Hibs had conceded the first leg in Greenock 0–1. Thus, thanks to Isak's goals, Hibs marched into a semi-final clash with Aberdeen.

A nippy, deep-lying, centre forward, Refvik signed on amateur forms until Hibernian acquired the then necessary work permits. Sadly, the twenty-two-year-old Refvik had insufficient international appearances to convince the government office involved that he merited a work permit and thus began a long, tortuous and ultimately fruitless wrangle between Hibernian and the authorities.

Hibs were livid at the time, particularly chairman Tom Hart, who viewed the whole proceedings as unfair on Hibernian, who had shown the vision to spot a couple of talented foreign players and snap them up before they became fully established internationals (and doubtless more expensive).

All the backing of the SFA and Players' Union was to no avail and eventually both Refvik and his compatriot Sven Mathison headed back to Norway. It was all down to timing – in years to come players arguably less talented, such as Peter Guggi, Alex Marinkov, Fabrice Henry and Hakim Sar Temsoury, would obtain a peg at Easter Road with little hindrance.

Refvik's final game in Hibs' colours was in the League Cup semi-final against Aberdeen at Dens Park. On that night, despite the backing of a huge Hibs support, the club slipped to defeat when Stuart Kennedy scored with a bizarre lob from the wing in the 107th minute. It was a sad end to the Norwegian affair but perhaps fitting in that there was an element of the bizarre – after all the whole business had been most unusual.

Isak returned to Viking and eventually totalled 407 games for his favourite club. Svein Mathisen, incidentally, went back to Start where he stayed from 1979 to 1989.

Appearances: 5 Goals: 0

REID Alan

Signed in July 1998 from Renfrew Victoria, he was a talented little midfielder who played his first game against Airdrie in the promotion-

winning season. He managed sporadic outings over the next few campaigns but ultimately sought an extended run to show his strengths. When Tony Mowbray arrived at the club the time was right for Alan to move and he joined Inverness Caledonian Thistle.
Appearances: 30 Goals: 1

REID Chris

Born in Edinburgh in 1971, Chris joined Hibs in May 1988. Standing 6ft 1in, he was a talented young goalkeeper but unable to oust either Andy Goram or John Burridge from the number one jersey. Capped by Scotland at Under-21 level, he joined Hamilton Accies in the 1998 close season but suffered a bad injury on his debut there.
Appearances: 35 Goals: 0

REID David

Played a couple of games in Hibernian's disastrous 1979/80 relegation campaign. His debut came against Morton in a 1–1 draw at Cappielow Park.
Appearances: 2 Goals: 0

REILLY John

In the mid-1960s John played two games for Hibernian in the League. He was an Australian and eventually was capped 15 times by his country but joined Hibs from Highland side Inverurie Locos. After playing with Hibs he served Washington and Melbourne clubs.
Appearances: 2 Goals: 0

REILLY Lawrie

Was this the greatest Hibee of them all? Most would say 'yes'. A legendary centre forward and a gentleman to boot, he was a Hibs hero from 1947 until his retirement in 1958. How ironic that just as he faded from the scene a lad called Joe Baker came into the team. Had Hibs been able to field both then surely no defence would have been safe.

Born and raised in Edinburgh, Reilly cut his teeth at juvenile level with North Merchiston and Edinburgh Thistle before joining Hibs. He made his debut when only seventeen but was very much a fringe player when the title went to Easter Road in 1948. When Willie Ormond was ruled out with a broken leg, the chance came for Lawrie to step into the side and he made such a good job of being an outside left that Scotland capped him in that position.

Eventually the more experienced Ormond returned and Lawrie was tried at centre forward… and the rest, as they say, is history.

Reilly shone as a centre forward. In season 1950/51 he scored 23 League goals and in the next six seasons he netted 27, 30, 15, 15, 23 and 16 League goals. He thus became the first Hibs player to top the Easter Road scoring charts in seven consecutive seasons. His haul of 30 League goals in season 1952/53 was a club record at that time.

Physically Reilly was not the archetypal centre forward. He was not particularly big, standing at just 5ft 7in, nor was he particularly heavy. Yet Lawrie was a prolific marksman and scored a good number of goals from headers. His explanation was that the other members of the Famous Five delivered telling crosses and passes. Were he less modest he would have mentioned his own sense of timing and sheer bravery.

Reilly could be a terror to individual teams. He scored seven against Motherwell in the two matches in season 1952/53. But like Ormond and Smith his run of success was halted by illness. He was diagnosed as having pleurisy in 1954 and missed the World Cup, although on reflection he may consider himself lucky to have avoided that dreadful trip.

Despite that 1954 setback he was an international hero and the darling of the famous Hampden slopes. Scotland's top scorer for three consecutive seasons, he also played five times for Scotland at Wembley and hit five

Lawrie Reilly.

goals… an astonishing feat. It was one of his international goals, a dramatic late counter in 1953, which effectively sealed the 'Last Minute Reilly' tag.

However, the 'last minute' title did detract from the real facts, which were that Reilly was a handful throughout the ninety minutes. How else could he have bagged no fewer than 22 goals in his 38 internationals? One cannot help but wonder how Scotland would have fared had they tried the entire Famous Five in one international, but it never happened. Four, minus Turnbull, did play in a Scottish League international in 1952 and Scotland won 2–0.

The final word on Lawrie Reilly's remarkable career must be that he was forced to retire when aged only twenty-nine.
Appearances: 253 Goals: 187

RILEY Paul

A single outing as a substitute in the 1996/97 season against Motherwell was the extent of Paul's career at Easter Road. A young midfielder, he had joined the club from Hutcheson Vale in August 1992.
Appearances: 1 Goals: 0

RENWICK Michael

Signed from Huchison Vale BC in August 1992, Michael was a redheaded full-back. He was quick and alert going forward and after making his bow in the Premier League he was part of the side that won the First Division Championship in 1999.

However, he was less able to hold down a first-team berth when Hibs rejoined the elite and moved down to the First Division with Ayr United. His debut for Hibs had been against Kilmarnock on the final day of the 1994/95 season.

He linked up with former Hibees Keith Wright and Mickey Weir at Cowdenbeath in 2002.
Appearances: 46 Goals: 0

Michael Renwick.

RICE Brian

This red-haired midfielder broke into the Hibs side with such devastating effect in the 1980s that he was soon on his way to the English First Division with Nottingham Forest. Born in Bellshill, Brian graduated from youth to Under-21 level for Scotland very quickly and as such was always going to be hard to hold on to.

He made his Hibs debut in an East of Scotland Shield final against Hearts at Tynecastle and stunned all and sundry with a magnificent goal from 25 yards. That piece of skill was in every sense a taster of what was to come from a very composed and creative midfielder.

Brian scored another cracker in a 3–3 draw at Dundee United in March 1983 and in season 1984/85 missed only one match all term.

Derek Riordan.

He was sold to Nottingham Forest for £175,000 in August 1985. Brian was on duty for Nottingham Forest on the day of the Hillsborough disaster. It was on 15 April 1989 that Liverpool met Forest at Sheffield Wednesday's ground and, in the worst stadium disaster to befall British football, ninety-six people died in a crush.

He came back to Scotland to play with Falkirk and then coached at both Clyde and Dunfermline before becoming assistant manager of Morton. The end of his career proved most interesting as he joined Ian McCall when Airdrie battled back from receivership in March 2001, prior to ultimately folding.
Appearances: 84 Goals: 11

RIORDAN Derek

Signed in 1999 from Hutcheson Vale BC, Derek had played alongside Garry O'Connor in Under-11 football and this helps explain the near telepathic understanding they had.

A scoring sensation in Hibs Under-18 and Under-21 sides, Derek made a most impressive first-team debut in the derby against Hearts in December 2001. Although slightly built he possessed great balance, a quick turn of speed and an astute footballing brain.

Initially unable to break into the first team under Bobby Williamson, he was loaned out to Cowdenbeath (along with Paul Hilland) and scored a quite sensational hat-trick as the Fife club won a remarkable game 7–5 at Brechin in January 2003.

He returned a better player and began to impose himself more on the first team. His splendid goal against Livingston, direct from a free-kick, got his scoring career underway and he was a regular marksman by 2004.

He was Hibs' top scorer in 2004 with 15 League goals and continued in that vein in 2005, so much so that he was repeatedly voted Scotland's Young Player of the Month.
Appearances: 50 Goals: 18

RIPPA Juha

On 16 November 1996 Juha made his only outing as a Hibernian player. Remarkably, it was in the Edinburgh derby at Tynecastle. Hibernian squeezed out a 0–0 draw but it was to little avail for Rippa, who never donned the green and white jersey again.

A twenty-eight-year-old midfielder, he was a Finnish trialist and had won a championship medal with FC Jazz. Still, his single outing was one more than the superbly named Casper Gribskjolo who arrived on trial at the same time.
Appearances: 1 Goals: 0

ROBERTSON Malcolm

He was signed on a three-month trial period by Pat Stanton in 1983. However, Malky was in the twilight of his career having enjoyed his best football while with Ayr United and Hearts.
Appearances: 5 Goals: 0

RODIER Derek

Was with Hibs in the late 1970s and early '80s. A centre forward, he combined his footballing duties with full-time study at Edinburgh University.

Derek was a useful marksman and a good leader of the line but arguably lacked the experience that Hibs required in this particularly testing era. He was clearly drifting out of the picture when Hibernian were relegated in 1980. He later played with Dunfermline.
Appearances: 31 Goals: 0

ROLLO Jim

This young goalkeeper made just two outings as a Hibernian player. These were in season 1955/56 but he was never able to cement a first-team place. Fortunately he had more joy with Oldham, Southport and Bradford City.
Appearances: 2 Goals: 0

ROSS Louis Alexander

A one-game career as far as Hibernian was concerned, his only outing came in the 1946/47 season, the first official campaign after the war. Like many players of his era his career was badly interrupted by the conflict – he had actually joined Hibs on 30 March 1940. He was transferred to Queen of the South on 1 October 1947 and also spent time with Walsall.

Appearances: 1 Goals: 0

ROUGH Alan

Born in Glasgow in 1951, Alan Rough was one of the finest post-war Scottish goalkeepers. It was Hibs' good fortune to have the services of the man affectionately nicknamed 'Scruffy' in the early 1980s.

Alan's distinguished senior career began in Glasgow with Partick Thistle and he made 410 League outings for the 'Jags' and established himself as Scotland's number one before Hibs bought him in November 1982 for £60,000. After 175 League outings it was clear that Hibernian had picked up a real bargain.

The owner, at times, of an exotic perm, Alan was capped 53 times by Scotland and was a participant in three World Cup finals. He was not unfairly given the lion's share of the credit for keeping Bertie Auld's unlikely Partick side in the Premier League. He also won a League Cup winner's medal with Thistle in 1971 (an unforgettable 4–1 triumph over Celtic).

His marvellous reflexes and wonderful sense of positioning were credited with many of the points Hibernian managed to collect during the cautious reign of Bertie Auld. He later played in America and with Celtic, Hamilton and Ayr United before moving into Ayrshire Junior football, where he managed Glenafaton Athletic.

Alan was the Hibs goalkeeper in the infamous clash with Rangers when Graeme

Alan Rough.

Souness was sent off. As virtually every player became embroiled in a fracas in the centre of the field, one scribe noted that Rough was watching, arms folded, from a distance. 'See Rough; he comes off his line for nothing!' he remarked.

Tony Rougier receiving a magazine award.

He was capped twice by Scotland while a Hibee, against England and Wales in 1986, the latter being interesting in that it was a World Cup qualifier and he replaced Jim Leighton (later to be a Hibs goalie too) at half time. Sadly the game will be forever remembered not for Scotland's World Cup progress but for the tragic death of legendary manager Jock Stein shortly afterwards.
Appearances: 175 Goals: 0

ROUGIER Tony

Signed from Raith Rovers during the summer of 1997 as Keith Wright and Ian Cameron went to Kirkcaldy, it was easy to see why Hibernian wanted Rougier. He had power, pace and an eye for goal.

A Trinidad & Tobago international, Tony had joined Rovers in March 1995 from Trinity Pros in Trinidad. He helped Rovers win the First Division Championship and was something of a cult hero in Kirkcaldy.

He left Hibernian for Port Vale when the club found itself in Division One and later played with Reading.
Appearances: 45 Goals: 4

S

SAR TEMSOURY Hakim

Alex McLeish loved to dabble in the transfer market and young Hakim was one of his bolder steps. He had a substitute outing at, of all places, Celtic Park in 2000 but failed to set the heather on fire and was allowed to return to France shortly thereafter.
Appearances: 1 Goals: 0

SAUZEE Franck

Raised in the small French fishing village of La Begude near Marseille, Franck was just seventeen when he joined Sochaux. He spent

Alex Marinkov and Franck Sauzee.

five very happy years there and was part of the French Under-21 side that won the European Championship. After 'cutting his teeth' he then moved to Marseille and, although he had a single year with Monaco, he returned to Marseille to help in the winning of the French League and Cup double in his first season. The highlight, however, was winning the European Cup in 1993 against AC Milan in Munich.

From Marseille, which suffered financially in the wake of owner Bernard Tapie's fall from grace, he joined Atalanta Bergamo in Italy; signed by the renowned Marcello Lippi. Things did not work out in Italy for Franck and he was sold to Strasbourg and stayed there until he was thirty-one, when he moved to Montpellier.

He was thirty-three years old and in dispute with his club when Alex McLeish persuaded him to join Hibernian. For such a player to come to Easter Road would at one time have been unimaginable. It was not just as a star in French domestic football that Franck had shone. He had 39 caps for France and had scored 9 goals. He was, in short, a top class international footballer.

Signed in 1999, while Hibs were in the First Division, Franck revelled in the freedom and responsibility he was given at Easter Road. He helped the club win that First Division in 1999 and in 2001 led the club out for the Scottish Cup final against Celtic.

Sauzee had all the skills of a top international star. He could play in midfield or as sweeper with equal impact. His long-range passing was awesome, as was his ability from the dead-ball situation; some of his goals for Hibernian were quite thunderous efforts.

He genuinely loved his spell as a Hibs player and put much of that down to the mature way in which Alex McLeish handled him. At one point, Alex devised an 'open plan' training schedule for the French master. Franck told me at the time: 'I prefer playing and live for the Saturdays. I am lucky at Hibs, however, as Alex McLeish and Andy Watson are so intelligent and recognise that I am thirty-four years old. They know that I need a different training schedule from the young players of say eighteen and nineteen. Sometimes when I am tired I have a rest and this is better for the team and for me obviously. I am grateful that the club recognise my situation.'

Alas, when Hibs boss Alex McLeish moved to Rangers, Franck was placed in the managerial chair. This was the natural move and it would have been ludicrous for Hibernian not to have offered the post to such a huge international star on their own pay-roll. However, things did not work out and after a sad few months (69 days in total), in which the nadir was losing to First Division Ayr United in a Hampden League Cup semi-final, Franck was sacked as boss.

Franck was a very personable man. As programme editor I had the task of speaking to Franck on Monday nights as we put together his programme notes. Initially these chats were a pleasure and his genuine passion for Hibernian shone through. However, as ignominious results heaped the pressure on he became withdrawn, beleaguered and almost perplexed.

For a man used to success as a player and clearly possessed of a wonderful mentality he found such a run particularly hard to bear. The image of him before the press under the main stand at Hampden Park after the League Cup semi-final exit to Ayr Untied was painful to behold.

Best to remember him as the truly legendary player he was. The song that rolled down from the terraces – 'There's only one Sauzee' – is the more fitting memory of a wonderful talent.

Appearances: 77 Goals: 13

SCHAEDLER Erich

In two spells with Hibernian, Erich became a cult hero. A solid full-back, he had tremendous fitness and was guaranteed to give 100 per cent week after week.

Erich had started out with Peebles Rovers and Melbourne Thistle before joining Stirling Albion, and it was from the latter that he joined Hibs in 1969. By the time the Turnbull's Tornadoes era was off and running in the early 1970s, the full-back pairing of Brownlie and Schaedler was a solid foundation in the Hibs team.

To Erich's two spells with Hibernian can be added stints with Dundee and Dumbarton. Erich was capped by Scotland, while a Hibee, against West Germany in 1974. He won a League Cup medal with Hibs and played in the Scottish Cup final in 1971.

Erich Schaedler.

While at Dundee he contested a League Cup final and picked up a First Division Championship badge. Tragically, Erich died in 1986 when aged only thirty-four. His parents were German but he himself was born in Biggar, where his father had been a prisoner of war.

Appearances: 299 Goals: 2

SCHMUGGE Thorsten

A German midfielder, Thorsten made just one outing as a Hibee, and that was as a substitute. The match in question was against Aberdeen at Pittodrie in September 1996 and Hibs recorded a fine 2–0 win thanks to goals by the deadly duo of Keith Wright and Darren Jackson.

A second-half substitute, the right-sided midfielder, who had played with Bochum and won German Under-21 caps, was promptly booked and thus made his one and only Hibernian appearance that little bit more noteworthy.

Appearances: 1 Goals: 0

SCOTT Alex

A dazzling winger as a youngster, Alex earned fame at Rangers, whom he joined in March 1955. He won four League Championship medals and 11 Scotland caps before moving to Everton in 1963. While at Goodison he added to his honours collection, winning both League and FA Cup medals and continuing his Scotland career.

In September 1967 he became a high profile Hibs signing and, although clearly in the veteran stages of his career, he still showed occasional flashes of brilliance. He ended his senior career in his home town of Falkirk. His brother Jim also played with Hibs and the two were, at one point, business partners in Falkirk.

It is worth reiterating that the Scott brothers did not play together at Easter Road or

Alex Scott.

Brockville, despite the proximity of their careers there.

Appearances: 16 Goals: 2

SCOTT Ally

A tall, strong-running forward, Ally seemed to fall between two stools and it was never quite clear if he was a winger who enjoyed playing inside, or a centre forward who drifted wide. He had started his career at Glasgow University and Queen's Park and then spent a couple of years at Rangers before joining Hibernian in the deal that saw Ian Munro head to Ibrox and Graham Fyfe journey to Edinburgh.

In the 1976 League Cup campaign he was among the goals and his clever, often speedy play served Hibs well for a short period.

After his stint at Easter Road Ally moved to Morton, and in truth he was a much better player in Benny Rooney's doggedly determined side than he had been in the green and white of Hibs.

Appearances: 38 Goals: 4

Ally Scott.

SCOTT Jim

Brother of the aforementioned Alex, Jim was twice capped by Scotland while a Hibee. He had joined Hibs in October 1958 from Bo'ness United.

Born in Falkirk in August 1940, he stood at 5ft 8in and – although not the strongest – he had an uncanny sense of balance. A clever player he could 'thread the needle' with his accurate passing and was equally capable of beating a man and homing in on goal.

He was famously one of two Hibs players to score four goals in an 11–2 rout of Alloa in September 1965, the other being Neil Martin. Between 1958 and 1967 he clocked up 172 League outings as a Hibee and scored 48 goals.

In August 1967 he was sold to Newcastle United and, while on Tyneside, he won a Fairs Cup medal when United annexed the 1969 trophy. Later in his career he played for Crystal Palace and Falkirk before retiring and buying a bar in his home town.

Jim's brother, Alex, also played for Hibernian, but not at the same time.

Appearances: 194 Goals: 48

Rab Shannon.

SHANNON Rab

Started his career with Dundee and stayed there for more than 250 matches in nine years before moving to Dunfermline. It cost Dunfermline two players (Ian McCall and Eddie Gallacher) plus £125,000 to move him. A former Under-21 cap, he was versatile enough to play either in midfield or as a full-back. He

then played for Motherwell for several years before making a 1996 move to Hibernian. It said much for the faith the Hibernian board had in caretaker boss Jocky Scott that they allowed him to spend £100,00 on Rab's signature. He survived the Jim Duffy era but Rab featured only once under Alex McLeish, during an injury crisis at Clydebank. Shannon's career came to an end with a stint as player/manager of East Fife.
Appearances: 6 Goals: 0

SHAW Davie

In 1939 David Shaw joined Hibs from Grange Rovers and, as the date suggests, his subsequent career would be interrupted by the Second World War.

A full-back who could play either right or left-back, he built a wonderful partnership

Davie Shaw.

with Jock Govan and both players won a Championship medal in 1948 after losing in the Scottish Cup final to Aberdeen one year earlier. Indeed, Davie captained Hibs to the 1947/48 title.

He left Easter Road in 1950 to join Aberdeen and played for the Dons until 1953. Upon hanging up his boots he joined the coaching staff and he worked in various capacities at Pittodrie until 1967.

Twice Shaw featured for Scotland in sides with two Hibernian full-backs. The first occasion was in April 1948 when he paired with Jock Govan against England and then in October he lined up alongside Hugh Howie for a rare Hibs double. As if that were not a good enough story then consider the fact that he had taken over from his brother (Jock) at full-back, a rare international feat indeed! His older brother was the legendary Jock 'Tiger' Shaw of Rangers.

He died in October 1976 when aged only sixty and had spent his final few years working in a paper mill near Aberdeen. Born in Annathill, Davie had worked as a miner before joining Hibs in January 1939.
Appearances: 85 Goals: 0

SHEVLANE Chris

Signed by Bob Shankly in the summer of 1968, redheaded Chris was a full-back who had been capped by Scotland at Under-23 level but had been surprisingly released by Celtic.

He went on to make 65 outings as a Hibee between 1968 and 1971. He picked up a League Cup runners-up badge while at Easter Road, which complimented an earlier medal gained with Hearts.

His capture was something of a coup in Edinburgh as he had started his career at Tynecastle and played for seven years with Hearts before moving to Celtic after apparently retiring through injury.

Chris Shevlane.

He did not succumb to injury however, but went to Celtic and then on to Hibs. In 1971 Hibs freed him and he moved to Morton, where he stayed until 1973.
Appearances: 65 Goals: 1

SHIELS Dean

Dean could have joined several clubs as a youngster but the young Irish striker opted for Arsenal and this gave him the chance to learn his trade alongside men like Thierry Henry, Robert Pires and Partick Vieira. Signed as a trainee in the summer of 2001, he was given a full professional contract by Arsene Wenger just twelve months later.

A prolific marksman for Arsenal at youth level he was understandably frustrated by the lack of first-team openings. In fact he was restricted to just two first-team pre-season friendlies in his time as a Gunner.

Tony Mowbray signed him for Hibs in July 2004 and, despite being only nineteen, he quickly made a big impression at Hibs. He was a noted marksman for Northern Ireland in the 2004 Milk Cup – he included Brazil among his victims and thus became the first Northern Ireland player at any level to score against Brazil.

SHIELDS Jay

A diminutive midfielder, Jay was a product of the Hibernian youth system and got a brief chance under Bobby Williamson. Born in Edinburgh in 1985, he was thus only nineteen when he made his debut at Livingston late in the 2003/04 season.
Appearances: 1 Goals: 0

SIMPSON Ronnie

One of the most remarkable stories in post-war senior football belongs to Ronnie. Here was a man who made his club debut as a four-teen-year-old and his Scotland debut as a thirty-six-year-old.

Born in Glasgow, he joined Queen's Park as a schoolboy and made his League debut for them against Hibernian in August 1946, but he had already kept goal for the Spiders in a first-team game as a fourteen-year-old. He stayed at Hampden for five years before making the short journey over the hill to Third Lanark and then on to Newcastle United.

He won two FA Cup winner's medals with Newcastle and was twenty-nine when Hugh Shaw signed him for Hibernian in October 1960.

Agile and a good shot stopper, he was very popular at Easter Road but did not get on with Jock Stein (who took over from Shaw) and left for Celtic. Imagine his horror then when Stein duly arrived as Celtic boss a few months later!

However, there was an extremely happy ending to this story. Stein and Simpson became reconciled and shared in the remarkable Lisbon Lions triumph as Celtic won the European Cup (and indeed everything they entered) in 1967.

Ronnie's father, Billy, had been a centre half with Rangers, so quite clearly, given Ronnie's long Celtic association, there must have been some interesting family discussion in the Simpson household.

Appearances: 123 Goals: 0

SIMPSON Billy

Signed from Edina Hibs in 1963, he managed a clutch of games in the mid-1960s. However, after little over forty appearances in seven seasons he moved to Falkirk and from there on to Albion Rovers, Alloa and Cowdenbeath.

Appearances: 45 Goals: 0

SKINNER Justin

A combative midfielder, Justin was signed by Alex McLeish at the tail end of the 1997/98 season as Hibs struggled in vain to stay in the Premier League.

The following season he played his part in helping the club gain promotion, but his aggressive style was never fully appreciated or admired by the Easter Road faithful. He was sent off along with ex-Hibee Gareth Evans in a 3–1 win at Airdrie in the autumn of 1999 as Hibs surged towards promotion and he tended to enjoy a 'stop-start' career in green.

He left Hibernian to join Dunfermline Athletic and served them for two years before joining Brechin City in August 2002. Prior to playing with Hibs he had served Bristol Rovers, Bournemouth, Wycombe and Wimbledon.

Appearances: 32 Goals: 2

SLAVIN Tommy

An inside left who joined Hibs in 1957 from Lesmahagow Juniors, he played two matches in the 1957/58 season.

Appearances: 2 Goals: 0

SMART Allan

A tall and rangy centre forward, Allan was signed on loan by Alex McLeish. The big striker managed a few outings, even scoring in a 4–0 win over St Johnstone, but generally failed to suggest he was any better than the players already on Hibs' books.

He later made a permanent move back to Scotland with Dundee United. While in England he had enjoyed some degree of success with Watford.

Appearances: 5 Goals: 1

SMITH Gary

When Alex McLeish offered Gary a short-term contract in July 2000, few could have imagined what an impact the former Scotland Under-21 international would make. 'Mr Consistency' would have been a fair title for Gary as he showed considerable experience in his defensive duties.

Gary could list Falkirk, Aberdeen (twice) and Rennes among his former clubs. His stint at Pittodrie, where Willie Miller and Alex McLeish had taken him under their wing, had proved particularly useful.

An unspectacular footballer, he settled well at Hibs and used his experience to good effect. Never a dirty player or a particularly outspoken one, he could nevertheless vent his fury when roused. Thus Gary had the rather unusual distinction of being sent off in successive matches against Rangers

Interesting to note that his move from Falkirk to Aberdeen in August 1991 was one of the first to be settled by transfer tribunal and the Dons had to pay £175,000 for the then twenty-year-old.

Appearances: 119 Goals: 0

SMITH Gordon

Gordon was arguably the greatest ever Scottish footballer. He joined Hibs in April 1941 and stayed until 1959. He won three League titles at Easter Road, then amazingly won Championship badges with Hearts and Dundee.

Gary Smith.

Gordon Smith.

An outside right, he was as elegant and athletic a player as has ever graced the Scottish football scene. He was born in Edinburgh in May 1924 and was a Scottish Schoolboy international before joining Hibs. He went on to win a host of Scotland caps and 10 League caps.

With Hibs he lost in both League and Scottish Cup finals, but with Hearts he won the League Cup. He retired from football in 1964 having played late in his career with Drumcondra in Ireland.

One of the great gentlemen of Scottish football, his name inevitably crops up whenever the more mature Scottish football writers speak of the truly magnificent players.

Signed in April 1941, Smith had caught the eye with Dundee North End and scored a hat-trick for a Scottish Junior select against a Hibs-Hearts eleven before his seventeenth birthday. Snatched from under Hearts' noses, the gifted youngster responded with a hat-trick for Hibs in a 5–3 wartime victory over Hearts on his debut. Thus began one of the greatest Hibs careers of them all.

With his ability to run at players with pace, and carry the ball beyond them, he was feared even as a youngster. He then benefited from playing in Hibs' wartime team, which frequently included experienced guests from south of the border, such as the legendary Matt Busby.

When football returned to normality after the war he was already evolving into an international class player. The icing on the cake was his ability to despatch chances with a powerful shot – a knack that made him the highest scoring winger in the history of the Scottish game. Smith was not only an effective player but also pleasing on the eye. He displayed great close control and supreme grace to baffle his opponents and was always a delight to watch, with many observers reckoning him to be the most charismatic player in Scotland.

His goalscoring became legendary and he rattled in 170 competitive goals for Hibs: there were 17 hat-tricks or better. When he topped the Hibs scoring charts in 1950, he capped a sequence that had seen him finish Hibs top scorer in seven out of eight seasons – not bad going for a wide player. He scored five in an 8–0 win over Third Lanark in 1947 and by the early 1950s was popularly appointed club captain.

In 1951 he was widely acclaimed as Scotland's Player of the Year. Two years on and Smith had reached the 100-goal mark for Hibs and clocked up his 500th appearance. A testimonial was richly deserved and a 7–3 win over Manchester United was the outcome in one of the most memorable games ever to take place in the capital city. Sadly he broke a leg in December 1953 and was lost to the game for several months. Injury it seemed was the only thing that could apply the brakes to a remarkable career. Yet he bounced back and, even in his mid-thirties, Smith was revered throughout Scotland and a popular choice as national captain in 1955.

Surprisingly, Hibs gave Gordon a free transfer in 1959 and he went on to win League Championship badges with both Hearts and Dundee… a truly remarkable feat. Never before, or since, has a player won Championship medals with three different clubs – none of them being based in Glasgow.

If evidence of Smith's remarkable fitness and longevity were needed then it surely came in the bald facts that he turned professional in 1941 and did not retire until 1964 – a twenty-three-year career! Sadly, Gordon passed away in 2004.
Appearances: 310 Goals: 126

SMITH Bobby

Born in Dalkeith in December 1953, Bobby joined Hibernian from Musselburgh Windsor in 1971. He was to have three spells with the club and was extremely influential in his first spell. A very versatile player, he was equally at home in midfield or at full-back.

Signed by Willie MacFarlane as a raw sixteen-year-old, Bobby almost joined Celtic. He told me: 'I was due to play for Celtic reserves on the Tuesday when Hibernian turned up on my doorstep the Sunday before and I was so impressed by their enthusiasm that I decided to join them.' He made his initial debut against Arbroath (as a substitute for the inimitable Jimmy O'Rourke) in November 1972 and his full-back exploits began in earnest when Erich Schaedler broke a collar bone in a match against Hearts.

He was very much a part of the Eddie Turnbull era (MacFarlane having departed) and in 1973 won a Dryburgh Cup winner's medal as Alan Gordon scored an extra-time winner against Celtic. Having made 152 appearances for Hibs, Bobby was ready for the move to English football, which came when Leicester City stepped in with an £85,000 cheque in 1978.

Bobby Smith.

He made his Leicester debut on New Year's Day 1979 and his spell in the East Midlands has to be termed a success as he twice won promotion from the old Second Division; a notable teammate was Gary Lineker. Bobby came back during Pat Stanton's reign in the early 1980s as a loan signing before returning to Leicester, where he found such good form that he was made club captain.

Bobby's third spell at Easter Road came when John Blackley signed him and it lasted until Alex Miller was appointed manager and set about revamping the playing staff.

From Easter Road Bobby moved to Dunfermline, Partick Thistle and Berwick Rangers.
Appearances: 153 Goals: 19

SMITH Tom

A bad injury ended Tom's career just as he was making himself a feature in the Hibs side at left-back.

Signed by Alex McLeish from Clydebank, Tom had been a Second Division Player of the Year and his career had started well with Partick Thistle.

Much of his Thistle football was played in the Premier League before he moved to Ayr United, where he won a Second Division Championship medal. It was then over to the Bankies, where he played only 22 matches before Hibs came calling in January 1999. He played only five games in the promotion campaign.

Appearances: 34 Goals: 0

SNEDDON Alan

Signed from Celtic in 1981 for a bargain £40,000, Alan won both Premier and First Division championship medals in his first season with Hibernian due to his split of games between Easter Road and Celtic Park.

Bertie Auld signed him and few could deny that Auld knew a good defender when he saw one. Sneddon, who was twenty-two when he joined Hibs, quickly justified the faith placed in him – although he did concede a penalty on his debut at Raith!

Alan Sneddon.

However, Hibernian were heading for promotion that season and Alan played his part alongside such veterans as Jackie McNamara and Ally MacLeod. There was a change of manager when Pat Stanton replaced Bertie Auld but Alan continued to play with his usual mix of determination and verve. This was also the case when Pat was succeeded by his former teammate John Blackley.

It was during this spell that Hibs knocked Celtic out of both the League and Scottish Cups. The former went to penalty kicks and required Roy Aitken to miss for the Bhoys and the latter saw Hibs win a seven-goal thriller by scoring twice in the last five minutes.

Such triumphs were not enough to keep John Blackley as Hibs boss when League form slumped and Alex Miller entered the manager's office. Soon Hibs were back in Europe for the first time in a decade. In all, Alan made over 300 League outings for Hibs and his reward came in 1991 when he enjoyed a testimonial match against Aston Villa.

Never a great goalscorer, he scored his first in Arthur Duncan's testimonial match – but in a League Cup tie in 1989 against Alloa, Alan scored twice in a 2–0 win!

A junior with Larkhall Thistle, Alan started his senior career in 1977 with Celtic and was signed by the great Jock Stein. He won a Scottish Cup winner's badge in 1980 and had the unenviable task of taking over at Parkhead from the truly legendary Danny McGrain. Highlights from his stint in the East End of Glasgow include helping the Celts beat Real Madrid 2–0 in 1980 and scoring for Celtic in a 2–2 draw at Rangers the very same year.

His career after Hibernian took him to Motherwell in July 1992. He made 16 League outings for the 'Well before bringing the curtain down on his senior career with a spell at East Fife.

Appearances: 312 Goals: 7

SOUNESS Jimmy

Best remembered for a four-goal salvo against Manchester City in a prestige friendly, he went on loan to Falkirk in January 1950 and joined Hearts in a permanent deal in January 1953.

He was something of a sporting all-rounder, enjoying both cricket and rugby in Edinburgh's thriving post-war sporting environment.

Appearances: 4 Goals: 3

SPALDING Derek

A young centre half who was given his debut in an East of Scotland Shield match, against Berwick Rangers in 1972. Born in Dundee, Derek had joined Hibs straight from school.

Dangerous at set pieces, he grabbed a couple of goals in Hibs' cup run of 1976 that saw replays aplenty. Derek travelled to America to play with Chicago Sting after his Hibernian career ended – which was convenient as he had married a girl from Chicago in 1975.

Appearances: 73 Goals: 1

STANTON Pat

It would be impossible to contemplate an 'all time greatest Hibees' list without including Pat Stanton. He played for the club between 1963 and 1976 and was quite simply a most accomplished performer.

Signed provisionally in 1961, Pat was farmed out to Bonnyrigg Rose before being called up in 1963 by Walter Galbraith. He made his debut against Motherwell in 1963 and scored in a 4–3 defeat.

His career never looked back and there were to be many highs in a Hibs jersey. He scored and captained the club to the 2–1 League Cup final win over Celtic in 1972 and was part of the side that mauled Hearts 7–0 on New Year's Day 1973.

The League Cup final was a seminal moment for the Turnbull era and Pat played a huge role. 'The achievement stands out,' he noted, 'because I don't think Hibs had won a cup in Glasgow for around seventy years. I scored a goal and it was a great feeling. Even although Kenny Dalglish pulled a goal back for Celtic, I actually thought we won that final far more convincingly than the 2–1 scoreline suggested.'

Yet he was quite clear about what he considered one of the best Hibs performances. It came in the European Cup Winners Cup in a second leg match. Hibs had lost 2–1 to Sporting Lisbon in Portugal but played sufficiently well to pave the way for an incredible 6–1 home triumph.

But Europe gave Pat his bitterest disappointment when Leeds United ousted Hibs on penalties after two goal-less draws. The shoot out ended up 5–4 for Leeds with Pat missing the first spot kick and retiring from penalty taking there and then.

The final sighting of Stanton in a Hibernian top came in August 1976 and a few days later he left Hibs to join Celtic having played in 399 league games.

The move to Celtic saw Pat win a League Championship medal and a Scottish Cup badge and in 1978 he returned to Easter Road for a testimonial match that was attended by over 20,000 appreciative fans.

When his playing career was over he moved into coaching as assistant boss at Aberdeen (to the famous Alex Ferguson) and success there earned him a move to Cowdenbeath as manager. From Central Park (after a mere 17 games) it was on to Dunfermline. He managed Hibernian in the early 1980s when the club nurtured promising youngsters such as Collins, Weir and Hunter, but in a period of transition Pat was unable to arrest a gradual decline.

Reflecting on that spell in charge later he would say: 'actually I did enjoy it although it was perhaps the wrong time to be in charge

Pat Stanton.

of the club. I was aware that it was a chance that might never come along again and I was desperate to take it when it emerged. The one aspect I certainly did enjoy was seeing a crop of good youngsters breaking through.'

The first former player I spoke to when I began writing the *Hibernian Match Magazine* was Pat Stanton and I must confess I was nervous about quizzing a man who had achieved so much in the game and was so thoroughly steeped in Hibernian history. I need not have worried, for Pat is among the most approachable men I have ever met. A wonderful ambassador for the club, Pat Stanton is one legend who fully lives up to the description.
Appearances: 399 Goals: 51

STEIN Colin

Born in Linlithgow in 1947, Stein joined Hibs in 1965 from Armadale Thistle. A bustling centre forward, he was only 5ft 9in but a very physical player nevertheless.

Noted for being the subject of the first six-figure transfer between Scottish clubs, Colin was a Hibernian hero in the mid-1960s. However, all that changed when he joined Rangers in October 1968 for £100,000 and promptly revealed his life-long support of the Glasgow club.

Nevertheless, nothing should detract from the good work Stein did while a Hibs centre. Brave, strong and very alert around goal, he was for several years the darling of the Easter Road terraces.

He was a natural goalscorer and had that selfish streak with which some forwards thrive. He certainly did not endear himself to officialdom and, while his disciplinary problems came to a head at Ibrox, they first surfaced at Hibs when he was sent off in 1968 against Raith Rovers.

As a Hibernian player he was capped by Scotland at League and Under-23 level. He led the line with vigour and scored several

Colin Stein.

sensational goals. Just how good a player he was can be gauged from the fact that he gave Leeds United's then England centre half Jackie Charlton a torrid evening in 1968 – when Stein scored and almost inspired Hibernian to a famous European win.

On his first outing for Rangers against Hibs he did what we all feared and scored a hat-trick in a 6–1 drubbing. Indeed, he seemed to enjoy playing against Hibs and scored the goal at Easter Road in March 1975 that won Rangers the final Scottish First Division title before the Premier League began. While at Rangers, with whom he had two spells, he scored in the 1972 European Cup Winners Cup final and earned the bulk of his 21 Scotland caps.

Colin later played with Coventry and Kilmarnock in a career that was liberally peppered with sendings-off and suspensions.
Appearances: 69 Goals: 40

STEVENS Tommy

Late in season 1972/73 Tommy made his debut in a match at Easter Road against Motherwell. Alas, it was his only League game for the club.

Appearances: 1 Goals: 0

STEVENSON Eric

An outside left, Eric joined Hibs from Hearts in 1960. He was with Hibernian for many years before moving to Ayr United in 1971, signed by another ex-Hibee, Ally MacLeod.

He formed an excellent partnership with Neil Martin at centre, the latter netting many of his headers from Stevenson's crosses.

Eric was raised in Bonnyrigg and, despite being a Hibs fan, he joined Hearts – only for the deal to falter at the eleventh hour. Hearts were to regret this in one particular derby when both he and Jim O'Rourke scored twice in the first ten minutes of a 4–0 win.

As John Campbell noted in the Hibernian match programme, Eric Stevenson could barely watch teammate Joe Davis taking

Eric Stevenson.

penalties. As Davis set himself to take the penalty, Stevenson had a habit of walking to the halfway line, near the dugout, before turning his back on play and crouching down and placing his forearms on his knees, waiting for the crowd reaction to see if we had scored. With Joe Davis an ace from the spot he was rarely disappointed.

Eric left Hibs to join Ayr United in 1971, ironically just as his early mentor Eddie Turnbull was returning to the club.

Appearances: 256 Goals: 53

STEVENSON James

Born in Bellshill in August 1946, James was a Scotland Schoolboy international. He was signed by Hibernian in August 1963 but managed only 13 League outings for the Hibees before falling out of the picture. He moved to Southend in July 1967 and played 33 League games for them.

Appearances: 13 Goals: 1

STEVENSON Maurice

An outside right, it was Walter Galbraith who had taken Maurice to Easter Road from Motherwell in May 1962. He gradually turned the former inside forward into a winger.

Maurice never really settled at Hibs and was moved on to Morton in July 1963. He had the last laugh against Hibs, being part of the Greenock side that surprisingly beat Hibs in the League Cup semi-finals of 1963.

From Morton he moved to Dundee United in the early 1970s. Perhaps most comfortable as an inside forward, he had skill and pace but lacked consistency.

Appearances: 20 Goals: 4

STEWART George

Edinburgh-born, George started his career with Tynecastle Boys Club then joined Dundee in 1964. His commanding displays

George Stewart.

won a band of admirers and it was no surprise when Hibernian finally lured him to Easter Road in 1976.

His move to Hibs coincided with Dundee's slip from the Premier League. A move to Edinburgh was ideal as he lived in the city and had a dry-cleaning business in Gorgie. He came to Hibs as a twenty-eight-year-old and formed a wonderful partnership in defence with firstly John Blackley and then Gordon Rae.

If every player has a defining match then it is likely that George's would be the 1979 Scottish Cup quarter-final tie against Hearts, when Hibernian not only won 2–1 but George headed one of the goals.
Appearances: 109 Goals: 2

STIRLING Robert

When you play two matches in your first season and score two goals you are entitled to think you have found your niche. Alas, this was not the case for Robert, who fleetingly

occupied a spot in Hibernian's first team in the 1946/47 season. His goals came in the last two games of the campaign, away to Third Lanark (unusually at Hampden Park) and Falkirk. Given that Hibernian lost the title by a mere two points he was unlucky not to celebrate a Championship success!

He had joined Hibs from Queen's Park and returned to the south side of Glasgow when joining Third Lanark.
Appearances: 2 Goals: 2

T

TEMPERLEY Willie

Willie came to Hibs in 1978 from Celtic having been an 'S' form signing at Parkhead. He therefore must have been a happy man indeed when he scored the goal that beat Celtic at Parkhead in September 1978. It was

Willie Temperley.

Hibs' first win there in nine years, so Temperley really did make the most of his return.

Appearances: 8 Goals: 1

THOMSON Darran

In the final two games of the disappointing 2002/03 season, Bobby Williamson gave Darran two outings knowing that he was going to release the player. The aim was to give him a shop window in which to show his talents and he took the opportunity fully, earning a move to newly promoted Inverness CT.

Appearances: 2 Goals: 0

THOMSON Kevin

Kevin made his debut early in the 2003/04 season. A left-sided midfielder, he showed remarkable composure for a young player. Prior to joining Hibs he had been with Hutcheson Vale and Coventry City.

His first goal was noted for being the winner in a 2–1 CIS Cup quarter-final triumph over Celtic late in 2003. Sadly, a cruciate ligament injury cost him the bulk of the 2004/05 season.

Appearances: 22 Goals: 1

THOMSON Jimmy

A left half, Jimmy made his first-team debut against Sheffield United in a friendly in March 1954. Indeed, he ended the season on a high and scored against Aberdeen in one of his three League outings that term. He was in and out of the side over the next few seasons and between 1953 and 1959 he played in 55 League games and contributed 8 goals.

Appearances: 55 Goals: 8

THOMSON Bobby

One of Scotland's more controversial, and dare one say it notorious, players, Bobby's downfall was a temper that was both swift and purposeful. Nevertheless, between the 'incidents' were some displays in both midfield and attack that were highly praiseworthy.

He began his career with Glasgow United and showed sufficient promise to earn a move to St Johnstone. He was a hit in Perth, bagging goals with rapidity.

He moved from St Johnstone to Morton for a Greenock record fee of £30,000 in July 1978 and the transfer was the making of him. He quickly won a Scottish League cap and Morton were able to turn down a £130,000 offer from Oldham Athletic for his services. Very versatile, he was comfortable playing as a striker or an attacking left-sided midfielder. However, he was plagued by indiscipline and frequently missed matches through suspension.

After playing with Middlesbrough, whom he joined in 1981, he journeyed to Hibernian and in 68 games was only sent off twice – but the second of those dismissals was one too many for the SFA, who slapped a six month ban on him.

His career with Hibs was followed by spells with smaller clubs such as Blackpool, Hartlepool, Hamilton and Queen of the South.

Appearances: 61 Goals: 12

TIERNEY Lawrie

Joined Hibs in March 1980 having spent several seasons with Hearts before drifting out of the game. A former Scotland youth international, he made his Hibs debut in a 3–0 defeat at Dundee. His stay at Easter Road was short and the midfielder soon returned to running his sandwich bar in the Roseburn district of Edinburgh. It was perhaps unfortunate that he arrived in the relegation campaign of 1979/80.

Appearances: 8 Goals: 0

Bobby Thomson.

TONER Willie

Born in 1928, Willie enjoyed an interesting and lengthy career, playing with Hibs from 1962 to 1963 and managing nine outings in that time.

His early clubs were St Paul's FC and Queen's Park before he joined Dundee. He then moved on to Sheffield United in May 1951. In 1953 he picked up a Second Division Championship medal with United and, when he came back to Scotland with Kilmarnock, he managed an outing in the 1957 Scottish Cup final. He repeated that feat in 1960 then joined Hibs in 1962.

Much was expected of Willie but he struggled to break into the side and Hibs only avoided relegation by two points in his first season. Worse was to follow in the next campaign as Willie made only one outing.

Not surprisingly he moved on, with Ayr United securing his services before he entered football management with Dumbarton.

Willie's son made his mark on Scottish football as a Grade One referee.

Appearances: 9 Goals: 0

TORRANCE Bobby

An attacking midfielder, Bobby was signed from St Mirren in March 1980. His career at Easter Road was short lived.

Nevertheless, he arrived with a sound reputation. He had indeed scored several goals against Hibernian in the course of a career that started at Anniesland Waverly. He scored twice on his Saints debut in a side managed by Alex Ferguson.

He left Hibs to join Partick Thistle, then had stints with Stirling Albion, Brechin City, Arbroath and Alloa. He continued his career as an apprentice quantity surveyor while with Hibs but when he gave the game up he opened his own travel agency and indulged his passion for scuba diving.

Appearances: 12 Goals: 1

TORTOLANO Joe

After two years as an apprentice at West Bromwich Albion, Hibs signed Joe in 1985. Capable of playing at full-back, in midfield or even out wide, he gained two Under-21 caps in 1987 against West Germany and Eire.

Joe was among the goals early in his career and went on to serve Hibs from 1985 to 1996. He played in 222 League games for Hibernian and while never a spectacular performer he did improve consistently and became a very important team player. Sadly he occasionally became a victim of the 'boo-boys' – a state of affairs that was hardly helped when he contrived to get himself sent off in a testimonial match against Manchester United (the foul incidentally against Gordon Strachan – a dyed in the wool Hibs supporter!). Joe later joined Stirling Albion, which was ideal as he lived a two-minute walk from their ground.

Appearances: 222 Goals: 13

TOSH Paul

Signed from Dundee by Jim Duffy in March 1997, there were high hopes for Paul Tosh. After all he was aged just twenty-three, stood at 6ft and had bagged goals aplenty for both Arbroath and Dundee.

A change of manager saw Jim Duffy give way to Alex McLeish and as the new manager brought in his own men it was clear that Paul was surplus to requirements. He spent a brief spell on loan to Partick Thistle and joined Raith and ultimately Forfar in permanent deals soon afterwards.

Tosh had arrived at Easter Road along with Lee Power from Dundee in March 1997 for a combined fee of £200,000.

Appearances: 22 Goals: 2

TOWNSLEY Derek

Standing at 6ft 5in, Carlisle-born Derek cut an imposing figure on the field. He was an apprentice at Carlisle United but left the

Paul Tosh.

senior ranks to play in the Unibond League with Gretna. He did well enough there to tempt Queen of the South and the highlight of his stay in Dumfries was a Challenge Cup final outing in 1997. Two years later he moved to Motherwell, where his versatility made him a valuable squad member.

Alex McLeish recruited Derek in July 2001 and he made his Hibs debut against Dundee in August of that year. However, he struggled to establish himself at Easter Road and arguably it took the arrival of Bobby Williamson to rescue a career that was drifting.

Under Bobby, the Townsley hunger was re-ignited and he responded with a clutch of goals. His composure, footballing awareness and willingness to run at defences gradually won over the Hibernian supporters and he ended the 2001/02 season with a glut of goals.

He scored in the remarkable 4–4 draw with Hearts in late 2002 but if his reactions were anything to go by he took greatest delight in nabbing goals against his former club Motherwell. The Fir Park faithful certainly appeared to have a thing about Derek!
Appearances: 43 Goals: 9

TURNBULL Eddie

Eddie was playing junior football in the Grangemouth area when he was recruited in 1946. A physically impressive man, he had the happy knack of possessing both aggression and creativity. What's more he was a thinking footballer and he followed a clutch of honours as a player with a raft of successes as a manager.

Born in Falkirk in 1923, he was to be the engine room of the Famous Five forward line. In his very first season with the club he tasted the drama of a Scottish Cup final and with his excellent workrate and thunderous shot he became a huge favourite with the Hibs fans.

When Willie Ormond arrived as outside left a partnership was forged that would last Hibs

a decade. Turnbull played as an inside left and became the enforcer for the lighter Smith and Ormond in a side that was high on flair but less so on aggression.

In February 1950 Turnbull stepped firmly into the limelight when he scored all four Hibs goals in a magnificent 4–1 Scottish Cup triumph over Celtic. Three of those goals were penalties and Turnbull had a routine approach to spot kicks – he simply blasted them.

Club captain by 1954, he was to win eight Scotland caps, one Scotland 'B' cap and four Scottish League caps to supplement his three League Championship badges. Indeed, the only item missing from his trophy cabinet was a cup winner's medal, despite playing in two Scottish Cup finals.

He addressed that absence as a manager. From coaching at Queen's Park he moved to Aberdeen and, in 1970, steered them to a Scottish Cup triumph over Celtic. When Tom Hart became Hibs' chairman he lured Eddie to Edinburgh in July 1971 and Hibs were suddenly on the up.

In 1972 the League Cup was won by Hibs, with Turnbull building a famous forward line of his own – Edwards, O'Rourke, Gordon, Cropley and Duncan. He forged Hibs into the second force in Scotland and had it not been for a powerful Celtic side they would have been the top club in the country. Nevertheless with Scottish Cup, League Cup and Dryburgh Cup final appearances and a 7–0 win over Hearts, Eddie more than did his bit for the club.
Appearances: 349 Goals: 148

TURNBULL Stuart

Could play either in defence or midfield and had done so for Dundee when Hibernian signed him in the early 1980s. He stayed at Hibs for three years, in which time he seemed to be little more than a fringe player. In 1984

Eddie Turnbull.

he moved on, joining Hamilton Accies – but he left there after only 15 League outings to take up a position with a club in South Africa. Upon retiring from playing he worked with Dundee United.

Appearances: 60 Goals: 1

TWEED Steven

A commanding central defender, Steven was signed in 1990 from Hutcheson Vale BC. He made his debut in 1992 against St Mirren and gradually forced his way into the first team. With the departure of Tommy McIntyre to Airdrie, the way seemed clear for 6ft 3in Steven to establish himself at Easter Road.

Alas, it did not work out that way and 'Tweedy' moved from Hibernian to Greece in 1996 and played with Ionikos before returning to Britain with Stoke City.

Jocky Scott, himself a former Hibernian manager (albeit as a caretaker), then took Steven to Dundee for £80,000 and the big defender did well to hold his place during the Bonetti revolution, which brought many overseas stars to Dens Park.

Appearances: 108 Goals: 3

V

VINCENT Stan

In February 1964 the club went to Cowdenbeath to sign a centre forward of some bulk. Although showing promise in flashes, he was unable to command an automatic spot so moved to Falkirk in order to secure a first-team berth.

Stan had scored 27 goals in 61 matches for Cowdenbeath and bagged 15 in 31 Hibs matches, which on reflection is a very useful return. His career with Falkirk was slightly less prolific, returning only 7 goals in 31 starts there.

There were short stints in South Africa and Northern Ireland (with Ballymena) before Stan returned to Easter Road to look after the third team for a short spell in 1971.

Appearances: 17 Goals: 8

W

WALDIE Simon

Signed in 1945 by Willie McCartney, Simon was a powerful centre half. He stayed with Hibs for five years before moving to Queen of the South. He was at Palmerston Park for a couple of seasons, playing against Hibs in a League Cup semi-final, before returning to the Highlands where he played with Ross County and worked with British Rail.

Appearances: 9 Goals: 0

WALKER Andy

Signed on loan from Sheffield United in December 1997, Andy was best known for his prolific scoring stints with Motherwell, Celtic and Bolton Wanderers. It is worth noting that Celtic paid £550,000 for him at his peak. Indeed, prior to joining Hibs he had scored 120 League goals and won three Scotland caps, but pride of place was probably his spell at Bolton, where he had scored 44 goals in just 67 matches.

He grabbed goals while at Hibs but no permanent move was forthcoming. Later in the same season he spent a period on loan to Raith Rovers and he netted a couple of First Division goals for them too.

From Sheffield United he made a permanent move to Ayr United in 1998, then followed spells with Carlisle, Partick, Kilwinning Rangers (where every game was postponed!) and finally Alloa Athletic. Upon retiring he moved into the media and proved a most able radio and television reporter.

Appearances: 8 Goals: 3

WARD Joe

Signed in 1979 from Aston Villa, Joe must be remembered as a player who threatened to score often but ultimately fell short of his own targets.

His list of clubs was extensive, including Clyde, Aston Villa, Dundee United, Ayr United, St Johnstone and Stirling Albion. He was given nine games in the 1979/80 season but failed to score in any of them.

Appearances: 9 Goals: 0

WARD Pat

Born in Dumbarton in December 1926, he made his Hibernian debut in the 1950/51 season as an energetic wing-half. Although he made 46 outings for the club, these were spread over five seasons and he was never an automatic first pick. He was sold to Leicester City in September 1955 and later played with Crewe Alexander. It was perhaps fitting that his career took him to England as one of his best performances for Hibs had been a friendly against Sunderland at Roker Park in 1954 when, on a snow covered pitch, he comfortably handled the legendary Len Shackleton.

Appearances: 46 Goals: 1

WATSON Andy

One of the select band of players to have served both Hearts and Hibernian, Andy eventually became assistant manager at Hibernian.

Born in Aberdeen in 1959, Andy was with the Pittodrie side for several years before joining Leeds United. Hibernian kept tabs on his midfield talents but it was Hearts who snapped him up for a £70,000 fee in 1984. Never fully appreciated by the Hearts support, he moved to Hibernian and gave solid service before beginning a coaching career that saw him work with Alex McLeish at firstly Motherwell, then Hibernian and latterly Rangers.

Appearances: 31 Goals: 3

WEIR Jock

Born in Fauldhouse in 1923, Jock joined Hibernian in 1942 and was a fine outside right. However, the development of the Famous Five meant Hibs could allow quite talented players like Weir, Alex Linwood and Leslie Johnstone to move on.

Nevertheless, his haul of 14 goals from only 19 matches in the 1946/47 League campaign suggests a player who could hold his own in most company. A nice recollection for Jock surely was that he bagged four goals in Hibernian's first post-war League match as Queen of the South were hammered 9–1 in a stunning return to action for the Hibees. Indeed that 14-goal total does not include a rich haul of cup goals that season, swelled by four strikes in a match against Alloa that Hibs won 8–0.

Jock moved to Blackburn Rovers in July 1947 for a record £10,000 but a year later was signed by Celtic for £7,000. He later turned out for Falkirk, Llanelly and Dumbarton.

Appearances: 19 Goals: 14

WEIR Mickey

Signed in 1982 by John Blackley, Mickey was a Hibs supporter whose love for the club in turn endeared him to the Easter Road support. A tricky winger, his diminutive stature did not hamper him in any way. He was a capable goalscorer, even with his head, and when in possession of the ball a buzz of excitement would sweep around Easter Road.

Standing at just 5ft 4in, Mickey made his debut in a League Cup tie in 1983/84 and two seasons later was regularly featuring on first-team duty. However, a contractual dispute in 1987 saw him head to Luton for £200,000.

He was unable to settle in Bedfordshire and for the same fee returned to Hibs just three months later. His second spell at Easter Road was arguably more profitable than the first and he played a major role in helping Hibs win the League Cup in 1991.

Mickey Weir.

He finally left Hibs in March 1997 to join Motherwell on a free transfer and scored against Hibs in a 6–2 reversal at Fir Park in January 1998 that ultimately cost Jim Duffy his job as Hibs boss.

At Fir Park Mickey graduated from playing to coaching and spent the bulk of his time with the younger players at Motherwell. By 2002 he was working as assistant manager to former Hibee Keith Wright at Cowdenbeath.
Appearances: 203 Goals: 30

WELSH Brian

Although born in Edinburgh, it was with Dundee United that Brian started his senior career. A powerful and towering centre half, he had the job of succeeding the likes of Gough, Hegarty and Narey at Tannadice and made over 100 appearances before moving to Hibernian in 1996.

His debut came against Kilmarnock at Easter Road but Hibs lost that game and soon afterwards Brian picked up the first of several injuries that curtailed his Hibs career.

One of his most memorable afternoons came at Fir Park, and it was not to be a good memory. Hibs were playing Motherwell in a vital relegation battle. Goals by Crawford and Lavety saw Hibs race into a 2–0 lead but a Motherwell fightback was helped by Brian being sent off when the score was 2–2. Garcin converted the resulting free-kick and Jim Duffy had his last game in charge as Motherwell went on to clinch a 6–2 win.

Brian did come back from this calamitous afternoon but he was released by Alex McLeish and began to drift down the leagues, playing with lowly Stenhousemuir at one stage.
Appearances: 34 Goals: 1

WELSH Peter

Played with Hibs during the 1982/83 season and had a League Cup goal before making a dozen League outings. Sadly his career was effectively over in 1983 due to a cartilage operation. Born in Coatbridge, he had arrived at Hibs from Leicester City.
Appearances: 12 Goals: 0

WHITTAKER Steven

Joined Hibs straight from school having played with distinction for Hutcheson Vale BC. He made his Hibs debut at the tail end of the 2001/02 season, away to St Johnstone as a substitute.

Steven was an overlapping wing-back whose skill and athleticism made him very popular. He came to the fore when the club embarked upon a cost-cutting exercise in 2003 and began to shed older players from the squad.

Steven Whittaker.

He scored his first goal against Partick Thistle in 2004 and was a regular in both the Scotland Under-21 side and the Hibs first team by that stage.
Appearances: 35 Goals: 1

WHYTE Hugh

A goalkeeper, Hugh was with Hibs in the mid-1970s but had to play second fiddle to Jim McArthur and eventually left to join Dunfermline Athletic.

A native of Kilmarnock, he joined from Hurlford United, turning down Crystal Palace and Huddersfield in favour of Hibs. He was part-time for most of his Easter Road career due to the fact that he was a medical student at Edinburgh University. He did graduate and at one time dovetailed his interests neatly by being club doctor at Dunfermline when his playing days were over.
Appearances: 5 Goals: 0

WILKINS Ray

A marvellously talented midfielder, Ray had been a star with England, Manchester United and AC Milan when he joined Hibs. Alas, he was most definitely in the twilight of his career when he came to Hibernian on a one-month deal in September 1996.

His list of previous clubs also included the likes of Paris St Germain and Rangers, so clearly Ray was as cosmopolitan as he was cultured. Few players could pass the ball with such unerring accuracy or control the midfield with such zeal and authority.

He had won 84 England caps by the time he joined Hibernian and it showed. His play was a delight to watch, measured and consistent, and although it was but a brief goodnight it was nevertheless immensely enjoyable to see such a talent at Easter Road.

Ray later managed QPR, worked on Channel 4's Italian football programme and as assistant manager at Millwall while continuing

to be a highly respected figure within the game.
Appearances: 16 Goals: 0

WILKINSON Ian

Played three times in 1968/69 and once the following season in his short Hibernian career. A wing half, his greatest difficulty was finding himself in opposition to the likes of Stanton, Blackley and Cousin. He did play with Hamilton Accies in the 1971/72 campaign.
Appearances: 4 Goals: 0

WILSON Mick

A midfielder, Mick played three matches in the 1975/76 season. However, he faced stiff competition for a first-team spot from men such as Des Bremner, Iain Munro, Alex Edwards and Bobby Smith. He left the club before the start of the 1977/78 campaign.
Appearances: 4 Goals: 0

WILSON Terry

Signed from Arbroath in 1980 under freedom of contract, Terry, who was a combative midfielder, ultimately cost Hibs £35,000. He had been with Aston Villa and Cowdenbeath before joining Arbroath and although a versatile player was best known as a full-back.

As a Hibs supporter he naturally enjoyed moving to Easter Road but in truth his transfer did not really work out. He lived in Dunfermline and was a part-time player working in the mining industry. His transfer to Hibs had a degree of controversy in that Hibs fielded Tommy in a reserve fixture with Aberdeen in the belief that he had earned a free transfer. This was not the case and he could not be properly signed until later.

He also played with Dunfermline, Dunedin (New Zealand) and Hamilton Accies in a fairly nomadic career.
Appearances: 7 Goals: 1

WILSON Willie

Although perhaps not the greatest ever Hibernian goalkeeper, there is no doubt that Willie featured in some of the most memorable Easter Road nights.

He was in goal when Hibs trounced Napoli (Dino Zoff and all) 5–0 in the Fairs Cup in 1967 and had kept a clean sheet against Real Madrid three years earlier.

Willie came from Wallyford and joined Hibs from Musselburgh Windsor in 1959. His debut was the stuff of nightmares, coming as it did in a 6–1 reversal against Rangers!

He vied with the likes of Lawrie Leslie and Ronnie Simpson for a first-team berth at Easter Road. When he did get in he showed himself to be agile and a fine shot stopper. He won a Summer Cup medal in 1964 but was also the 'keeper when Motherwell's Ian St John scored a hat-trick against Hibs in just 150 seconds.

When he retired from playing he continued his connection with football as an early example of the goalkeeping coach, working with Berwick, Falkirk and Hearts.

Appearances: 103 Goals: 0

WISS Jarkko

Signed from Stockport County in January 2002, Jarkko made his Hibernian debut as a substitute against Aberdeen in a 3–4 defeat at Easter Road. He was Franck Sauzee's second signing, following on from the arrival of Kevin Nicol of Raith Rovers. A full Finnish international, Jarkko had earned 38 caps and scored 3 goals.

He joined Stockport from Norwegian side Moss FK for £350,000 and, in 47 outings for the English club, scored times. Jarkko played with TPV Tampere and FF Jaro Pietarsaari in Finland before making his international debut against Denmark in February 1996. He sounded out ex-Hibee Mixu Paatelainen and Hearts' Finnish star Tommi Gronlund in the lead-up to his transfer to Hibernian.

Willie Wilson, sixth from right in the middle row.

It would be fair to say that he took time to settle at Easter Road in Bobby Williamson's side and there was little surprise when he returned to Tampere in 2004.
Appearances: 48 Goals: 0

WOOD Robert

Signed as a seventeen-year-old from Musselburgh Union, Robert was farmed out to Haddington Athletic before being called up by Hibs. He scored two goals in only five matches in the 1950/51 season and suggested there were more to come. The trouble was that other clubs agreed and Hibs reluctantly sold him to Barnsley in July 1951. This was a something of a mistake as he went on to make 336 appearances for the Tykes and bagged a very useful 41 goals. With Hibs he played as an inside forward but he moved to wing-half in South Yorkshire.
Appearances: 5 Goals: 2

WREN Jackie

John Mackie Wren, known as 'Jackie', was signed from Gairdoch Juveniles and made 31 outings between 1956 and 1960. He moved to Rotherham United in August 1960 but made only a single appearance as their goalkeeper. He signed for Dundee United in December 1962 but only played one reserve match before being released in January 1963.
Appearances: 31 Goals: 0

WRIGHT Alexander

Played two League games for Hibernian in the 1946/47 season but moved to Barnsley in August 1947 and served them well with 30 goals in 80 matches; sufficient to earn him a move to Tottenham Hotspur. That transfer never quite worked out and he went on to have greater success with Bradford Park Avenue between 1951 and 1954. He would later serve both Falkirk and Arbroath.

Alex was born in Kirkcaldy in 1925.
Appearances: 2 Goals: 0

WRIGHT Keith

When bought from Dundee in 1991 Keith was Hibs' record signing – it had taken a cheque for £500,000 to prise him from Dens Park. It was ironic he should cost half a million pounds because he had been an 'S' form signing at Easter Road but failed to make the mark.

He then played with Melbourne Thistle and in 1983 joined Raith Rovers. He became a scoring sensation in Kirkcaldy and grabbed 61 League goals in only 127 starts. In December 1986 he joined Dundee and while there he forged a wonderful partnership with Tommy Coyne. Keith managed 62 goals in his 167 League outings.

A lifelong Hibs fan, his July 1991 move to Easter Road was a dream come true. He scored 17 goals in his first season as a Hibee but pride of place was reserved for his League Cup performances and goals in the semi-final and the final brought the cup back to Easter Road.

So impressive was Keith as a Hibee that he was capped by Scotland (against Northern Ireland). From Hibs he moved to Raith Rovers then Morton. Keith brought the curtain down on his senior career with Cowdenbeath and by the start of the 2002/03 season was settled as the Fife club's manager.
Appearances: 197 Goals: 60

WRIGHT Paul

Born in East Kilbride in 1967, Paul joined Aberdeen as an 'S' form and showed great promise while at Pittodrie. First-team football and goals, however, did not come regularly enough and he moved to Queen's Park Rangers where he scored 5 goals in just 15 appearances. Despite this impressive impact, he could not settle in West London and Hibs snapped him up in a £250,000 deal in March 1990.

Capped by Scotland at Youth and Under-21 level, he made his Hibs debut against, of all

Keith Wright.

teams, Aberdeen and scored in a 3–2 win! Hibs beat Rangers 1–0 in the very next game but a 1–2 defeat to Hearts saw Paul pick up a bad injury and his season was over.

He bounced back in the 1990/91 campaign and was top scorer with 6 goals, but it was a disappointing season for the club and only the presence of a very ordinary St Mirren side prevented Hibs propping up the table.

In 1991 Paul was sold to St Johnstone for a record Perth fee of £285,000. Later in his career he played for Kilmarnock (he was their record signing too – this time at £330,000), Morton and Clydebank. While with Killie he won a Scottish Cup winner's badge – indeed, he scored the winning goal in the final. He was less fortunate at Clydebank, where the club eventually folded.

Appearances: 36 Goals: 7

Y

YOUNG John

A centre half, John made the bulk of his outings for Hibs in the 1959/60 season. It was clear however by 1962 that he was not an automatic first-team pick and after spending the summer with Toronto he joined St Johnstone.

He made only seven League outings for the Perth men before returning to Canada and Toronto.

Appearances: 41 Goals: 2

YOUNGER Tommy

A wonderful goalkeeper, Tommy won 24 Scotland caps and made a huge impression with both Hibs and Liverpool. Between 1949 and 1956 (his time at Easter Road) Tommy kept goal in 176 League matches.

Born in Edinburgh in 1930, he was signed from Hutchison Vale in 1948. Tall, golden-

Tommy Younger.

haired and thoroughly likable, his association with Hibernian was to be both lengthy and rewarding.

His debut came against Partick Thistle at Easter Road in April 1949 and he was in goal when Hibs lost the 1951 League Cup final rather surprisingly 3–0 to Motherwell. He recovered from that black day and had two championship medals to show for his time as a Hibee.

A cheque for £9,000 made out by Liverpool in June 1956 was sufficient to prise him away to Merseyside and as part of that deal Hibs met Liverpool in a floodlit friendly.

Later in his career he played with Falkirk, but in March 1960 he returned to England to play with Stoke City. He made only 10 outings for them but, following a stint in Toronto, Canada, joined Leeds United and played 37 League matches before coming home to settle in Scotland.

In 1970 he joined the Board of Directors at Easter Road and thirteen years on from that he was President of the SFA. Alas, he died in January 1984 when aged only fifty-three.

Appearances: 176 Goals: 0

Z

ZAMBERNARDI Yannick

Signed as a twenty-four-year-old by Bobby Williamson during Hibs' disastrous start to the 2002/03 season, he made his debut in a 1–2 defeat at Dundee.

There were two major features in his game. Firstly, he had a propensity to indulge in rash sliding tackles, but this was offset by his second habit – that of pinging long diagonal balls forward. Born in Ajaccio on the French island of Corsica, he started his senior career with Bastia. Yannick then moved to AC Ajaccio, where he impressed sufficiently to earn a move to Troyes, where he was a teammate of Freddy Arpinon.

His time at Easter Road will be remembered largely for his sheer enjoyment of sliding tackles: great when they came off, but leaving the defence hopelessly exposed when they were mistimed. He left Hibs in 2004 to join La Louvière in Belgium.

Appearances: 36 Goals: 0

ZITELLI David

A clever French striker who was lured to Easter Road by Alex McLeish… and the fact that his great friend Franck Sauzee was already on Hibs' books.

Zitelli had been a notable striker and had caught British attention when scoring UEFA

David Zitelli.

Cup goals against both Liverpool and Rangers.

His impact at Hibernian was significant. An early goal proved to be the winner against Rangers and he scored in the Scottish Cup semi-final win against Livingston. Spectacular goals were a speciality and counters against Dundee (at Dens Park) and Motherwell (at Fir Park) were absolute beauties. His powerful shooting and shrewd positional sense made him a dangerous striker and he scored in the 6–2 rout of Hearts and the never-to-be-forgotten UEFA Cup classic against AEK Athens.

David left Hibernian in the summer of 2002 and joined Istres in France, and Hibs fans were left wondering just what might have happened had the Zitelli prowess been available a few years earlier.

Appearances: 52 Goals: 10

HIBERNIAN MANAGERS

	In	Out
Dan McMichael	1903	1919
David Gordon	1919	1920
Alex Maley	1920	1925
Bobby Templeton	1925	1936
Willie McCartney	1936	1948
Hugh Shaw	1948	1961
Walter Galbraith	1961	1964
Jock Stein	1964	1965
Bob Shankly	1965	1969
Willie McFarlane	1969	1970
Dave Ewing	1970	1971
Eddie Turnbull	1971	1980
Willie Ormond	1980	1980
Bertie Auld	1980	1982
Pat Stanton	1982	1984
John Blackley	1984	1986
Alex Miller	1986	1996
Jim Duffy	1996	1998
Alex McLeish	1998	2001
Franck Sauzee	2001	2002
Bobby Williamson	2002	2004
Tony Mowbray	2004	

LEADING GOALSCORERS FROM 1946/47

(League goals scored per season up to 2003/04)

1946/47	Jock Weir 14, Eddie Turnbull 13
1947/48	Gordon Smith 19, Alex Linwood 14
1948/49	Lawrie Reilly 14, Johnny Cuthbertson 14
1949/50	Gordon Smith 25, Eddie Turnbull 18
1950/51	Lawrie Reilly 23
1951/52	Lawrie Reilly 27, Bobby Johnstone 23
1952/53	Lawrie Reilly 29
1953/54	Lawrie Reilly 15
1954/55	Lawrie Reilly 15
1955/56	Lawrie Reilly 23
1956/57	Lawrie Reilly 17
1957/58	Joe Baker 14
1958/59	Joe Baker 25
1959/60	Joe Baker 41
1960/61	Joe Baker 21
1961/62	Duncan Falconer 12
1962/63	Gerry Baker 13
1963/64	Neil Martin 20
1964/65	Neil Martin 25, Jim Scott 15
1965/66	Peter Cormack 15
1966/67	Peter Cormack 13, Joe Davis 13
1967/68	Colin Stein 21, Peter Cormack 11
1968/69	Joe McBride 19
1969/70	Joe McBride 20
1970/71	Joe Baker 8
1971/72	Jim O'Rourke 11, Arthur Duncan 11
1972/73	Alan Gordon 27
1973/74	Alan Gordon 16, Jim O'Rourke 14
1974/75	Joe Harper 12, Arthur Duncan 12
1975/76	Arthur Duncan 13
1976/77	Bobby Smith 8, Ally MacLeod 7

1977/78	Ally MacLeod 16
1978/79	Ally MacLeod 8
1979/80	Ally MacLeod 8
1980/81	Ally MacLeod 15, Gordon Rae 13
1981/82	Gordon Rae 11
1982/83	Gavin Murray 6, Gordon Rae 6
1983/84	Willie Irvine 19
1984/85	Gordon Durie 8, Paul Kane 8
1985/86	Steve Cowan 19
1986/87	George McCluskey 9
1987/88	Paul Kane 10, John Collins 6
1988/89	Steve Archibald 13
1989/90	Keith Houchen 8
1990/91	Paul Wright 6
1991/92	Mickey Weir 11
1992/93	Darren Jackson 13, Keith Wright 11
1993/94	Keith Wright 16
1994/95	Michael O'Neill 10, Darren Jackson 10, Keith Wright 10
1995/96	Keith Wright 10
1996/97	Darren Jackson 11
1997/98	Stevie Crawford 9
1998/99	Stevie Crawford 14, Pat McGinlay 12, Mixu Paatelainen 12
1999/2000	Kenny Miller 12
2000/01	Mixu Paatelainen 11, David Zitelli 10
2001/02	Garry O'Connor 9
2002/03	Tom McManus 12
2003/04	Derek Riordan 15

LEADING POST-WAR GOALSCORERS

(Goals scored in League games to the end of the 2003/04 season)

Player	Career	Appearances (Subs)		Goals
L. Reilly	1946–58	253		187
E. Turnbull	1946–59	349		148
W. Ormond	1946–61	348		133
G. Smith	1946–59	310		126
J. Baker	1957–61;1970–72	138	(1)	113
R. Johnstone	1948–55;1959–61	195		100
J. O'Rourke	1962–74	202	(8)	81
P. Cormack	1962–70;1979–81	197	(3)	77
A. Duncan	1969–84	436	(12)	73
A. MacLeod	1974–82	201	(7)	72
P. McGinlay	1988–2000	299	(23)	60
K. Wright	1991–97	184	(13)	60
R. Combe	1946–57	264		54
N. Martin	1963–66	65		53
E. Stevenson	1960–72	255	(1)	53
A. Gordon	1971–75	83	(1)	51
P. Stanton	1963–76	397	(2)	51
D. Jackson	1992–97	160	(12)	50

MOST LEAGUE APPEARANCES SINCE 1946/47

(Players who were ever-present in a League season up to 2003/04)

1946/47	None
1947/48	None
1948/49	None
1949/50	Jimmy Cairns, Bobby Combe, Willie Ormond
1950/51	Jock Paterson
1951/52	Jock Govan, Hugh Howie, Jock Paterson
1952/53	Bobby Combe, Bobby Johnstone
1953/54	Bobby Johnstone
1954/55	Willie Ormond, Jock Paterson
1955/56	None
1956/57	Eddie Turnbull
1957/58	None
1958/59	None
1959/60	None
1960/61	Johnny MacLeod
1961/62	Ronnie Simpson, Ally MacLeod
1962/63	None
1963/64	None
1964/65	Willie Wilson, Willie Hamilton
1965/66	Joe Davis, Pat Stanton
1966/67	Joe Davis, Bobby Duncan, Alan Cousin
1967/68	Joe Davis, Allan McGraw
1968/69	Joe Davis
1969/70	None
1970/71	None
1971/72	Jim Herriot
1972/73	Jim Black
1973/74	None
1974/75	Joe Harper, Pat Stanton

1975/76	Arthur Duncan
1976/77	Bobby Smith, Mike MacDonald, John Brownlie, Des Bremner
1977/78	Mike MacDonald, George Stewart, Ally MacLeod
1978/79	Ally MacLeod
1979/80	None
1980/81	Arthur Duncan
1981/82	Craig Paterson, Alan Sneddon
1982/83	Alan Sneddon
1983/84	Willie Irvine
1984/85	Alan Sneddon
1985/86	Steve Cowan, Alan Rough
1986/87	None
1987/88	Paul Kane, John Collins
1988/89	Andy Goram
1989/90	None
1990/91	None
1991/92	None
1992/93	None
1993/94	Jim Leighton
1994/95	Jim Leighton
1995/96	Jim Leighton, Darren Jackson
1996/97	None
1997/98	None
1998/99	Ole Gottskalksson
1999/2000	None
2000/01	None
2001/02	None
2002/03	None
2003/04	Daniel Andersson

APPENDIX V
LEADING POST-WAR APPEARANCES

(Total number of appearances up to the end of season 2003/04)

Player	Hibs Career	Appearances (Subs)		Total
A. Duncan	1969–84	436	(12)	448
P. Stanton	1963–76	397	(2)	399
E. Turnbull	1946–59			349
W. Ormond	1946–61			348
G. Rae	1977–90	337	(11)	348
G. Hunter	1983–97	333	(6)	339
P. McGinlay	1988–2000	299	(23)	322
A. Sneddon	1980–92	303	(9)	312
G. Smith	1946–59			310
E. Schaedler	1969–78; 1981–85	291	(8)	299
J. Paterson	1948–59			283
J. Blackley	1967–78; 1983–84	278	(1)	279
G. Mitchell	1986–96	258	(7)	265
R. Combe	1946–57			264
E. Stevenson	1960–72	255	(1)	256
L. Reilly	1946–58			253
P. Kane	1983–91	236	(11)	247
G. Evans	1987–96	166	(81)	247
W. Miller	1989–98	239	(7)	246
J. McNamara	1976–85	231	(5)	236
T. Preston	1953–64			228
John Grant	1954–64			225
J. Tortolano	1985–96	154	(68)	222
R. Callachan	1978–86	211	(8)	219
J. McArthur	1972–83			217
J. Brownlie	1969–78			211
J. O'Rourke	1962–74	202	(8)	210
J. Baxter	1957–66			209
A. MacLeod	1974–82	201	(7)	208
A. Buchanan	1946–57			205

M. Weir	1984–97	160 (43)	203
A. Brazil	1976–86	189 (13)	202
D. Bremner	1972–80		200
P. Cormack	1962–70; 1979-81	197 (3)	200
K. Wright	1991–97	184 (13)	197
J. Fraser	1954–66		195
R. Johnstone	1948–55; 1959–61		195
J. Scott	1958–68		194
B. Hamilton	1989–95	183 (11)	194
J. McClelland	1954–64		183
T. Younger	1949–56		176
A. Rough	1982–88		175
D. Jackson	1992–97	160 (12)	172
N. Orr	1987–93	151 (15)	166
J. Govan	1946–54		163
J. Collins	1985–90	155 (8)	163
J. Davis	1964–70		157
B. Smith	1972–79	131 (22)	153
J. Black	1969–74		151
J. Leighton	1993–97		151

COMPLETE LEAGUE RECORD

Season	Played	Won	Drew	Lost	For	Against	Points	Position
1946/47	30	19	6	5	69	33	44	2
1947/48	30	22	4	4	86	27	48	1
1948/49	30	17	5	8	75	52	39	3
1949/50	30	22	6	3	86	34	49	2
1950/51	30	22	4	4	78	26	48	1
1951/52	30	20	5	5	92	36	45	1
1952/53	30	19	5	6	83	51	43	2
1953/54	30	15	4	11	72	51	34	5
1954/55	30	15	4	11	64	54	34	5
1955/56	34	19	7	8	86	50	45	4
1956/57	34	12	9	13	69	56	33	9
1957/58	34	13	5	16	59	60	31	9
1958/59	34	13	6	15	68	70	32	10
1959/60	34	14	7	13	106	85	35	7
1960/61	34	15	4	15	66	69	34	8
1961/62	34	14	5	15	58	72	33	8
1962/63	34	8	9	17	47	67	25	16
1963/64	34	12	6	16	59	66	30	10
1964/65	34	21	4	9	75	47	46	4
1965/66	34	16	6	12	81	55	38	6
1966/67	34	19	4	11	72	49	42	5
1967/68	34	20	5	9	67	49	45	3
1968/69	34	12	7	15	60	59	31	12
1969/70	34	19	6	9	65	40	44	3
1970/71	34	10	10	14	47	53	30	12
1971/72	34	19	6	9	62	34	44	4
1972/73	34	19	7	8	74	33	45	3
1973/74	34	20	9	5	75	42	49	2
1974/75	34	20	9	5	69	37	49	2
1975/76	36	18	7	11	55	43	43	3
1976/77	36	8	18	10	34	35	34	6

1977/78	36	15	7	14	51	43	37	4
1978/79	36	12	13	11	44	48	37	5
1979/80	36	36	6	24	29	67	18	10 (R)
1980/81	39	24	9	6	7	24	57	1 (P)
1981/82	36	11	14	11	38	40	36	6
1982/83	36	7	15	14	35	51	29	7
1983/84	36	12	7	17	45	55	31	7
1984/85	36	10	7	19	38	61	27	8
1985/86	36	11	6	19	49	63	28	8
1986/87	44	10	13	21	44	70	33	9
1987/88	44	12	19	13	41	42	43	6
1988/89	36	13	9	14	37	36	35	5
1989/90	36	12	10	14	32	41	34	7
1990/91	36	6	13	17	24	51	25	9
1991/92	44	16	17	11	53	45	49	5
1992/93	44	12	13	19	54	64	37	7
1993/94	44	16	15	13	53	48	47	5
1994/95	36	12	17	7	49	37	53	3
1995/96	36	11	10	15	43	57	43	5
1996/97	36	9	11	16	38	55	38	9
1997/98	36	6	12	18	38	59	30	10 (R)
1998/99	36	28	5	3	84	33	89	1 (P)
1999/00	36	10	11	15	49	61	41	6
2000/01	38	18	12	8	57	35	66	3
2001/02	38	10	11	17	51	56	41	10
2002/03	38	15	6	17	56	64	51	7
2003/04	38	11	11	16	41	60	44	8
Totals	2045	847	497	701	3409	2901	2321	

Key:

(R) – Relegated

(P) – Promoted

COMPLETE SCOTTISH CUP RECORD

1946/47	Final	1975/76	Quarter-finals
1947/48	Semi-finals	1976/77	Round 4
1948/49	Quarter-finals	1977/78	Round 4
1949/50	Round 1	1978/79	Final
1950/51	Semi-finals	1979/80	Semi-finals
1951/52	Round 1	1980/81	Quarter-finals
1952/53	Quarter-finals	1981/82	Round 4
1953/54	Round 3	1982/83	Round 3
1954/55	Round 5*	1983/84	Round 3
1955/56	Round 5*	1984/85	Round 3
1956/57	Round 5*	1985/86	Semi-finals
1957/58	Final	1986/87	Round 4
1958/59	Quarter-finals	1987/88	Round 4
1959/60	Quarter-finals	1988/89	Semi-finals
1960/61	Quarter-finals	1989/90	Quarter-finals
1961/62	Round 1	1990/91	Round 4
1962/63	Round 3	1991/92	Quarter-finals
1963/64	Round 1	1992/93	Semi-finals
1964/65	Semi-finals	1993/94	Round 4
1965/66	Round 2	1994/95	Semi-finals
1966/67	Quarter-finals	1995/96	Round 3
1967/68	Round 2	1996/97	Round 4
1968/69	Round 1	1997/98	Round 3
1969/70	Round 1	1998/99	Round 3
1970/71	Semi-finals	1999/00	Semi-finals
1971/72	Final	2000/01	Final
1972/73	Round 4	2001/02	Round 4
1973/74	Round 4	2002/03	Round 4
1974/75	Round 3	2003/04	Round 3

*Note that over time the names given to rounds have altered; thus the fifth round of the 1950s, for example, is the equivalent to today's third round.

APPENDIX VIII
COMPLETE LEAGUE CUP RECORD

1946/47	Semi-finals	1975/76	Quarter-finals
1947/48	Section	1976/77	Section
1948/49	Section	1977/78	First Round
1949/50	Semi-finals	1978/79	Semi-finals
1950/51	Final	1979/80	Second Round
1951/52	Section	1980/81	Third Round
1952/53	Semi-finals	1981/82	Section
1953/54	Semi-finals	1982/83	Section
1954/55	Section	1983/84	Second Round
1955/56	Section	1984/85	Second Round
1956/57	Section	1985/86	Final
1957/58	Section	1986/87	Quarter-finals
1958/59	Section	1987/88	Quarter-finals
1959/60	Section	1988/89	Quarter-finals
1960/61	Section	1989/90	Quarter-finals
1961/62	Section	1990/91	Second Round
1962/63	Section	1991/92	Winners
1963/64	Semi-finals	1992/93	Second Round
1964/65	Section	1993/94	Final
1965/66	Semi-finals	1994/95	Quarter-finals
1966/67	Section	1995/96	Second Round
1967/68	Section	1996/97	Quarter-finals
1968/69	Final	1997/98	Second Round
1969/70	Section	1998/99	Quarter-finals
1970/71	Quarter-finals	1999/00	Second Round
1971/72	Quarter-finals	2000/01	Quarter-finals
1972/73	Winners	2001/02	Semi-finals
1973/74	Semi-finals	2002/03	Second Round
1974/75	Final	2003/04	Final

COMPLETE EUROPEAN RECORD

1955/56 – EUROPEAN CUP

Rd 1	Rot Weiss	(A)	W 4–0
Rd 1	Rot Weiss	(H)	D 1–1
Rd 2	Djurgaardens	(A)	W 3–1
Rd 2	Djurgaardens	(H)	W 1–0
SF	Rheims	(A)	L 0–2
SF	Rheims	(H)	L 0–1

1960/61 – FAIRS CUP

Rd 2	Barcelona	(A)	D 4–4
Rd 2	Barcelona	(H)	W 3–2
SF	Roma	(H)	D 2–2
SF	Roma	(A)	D 3–3
Replay	Roma	(A)	L 0–6

1961/62 – FAIRS CUP

Rd 1	Belenenses	(H)	D 3–3
Rd 1	Belenenses	(A)	W 3–1
Rd 2	Red Star	(A)	L 0–4
Rd 2	Red Star	(H)	L 0–1

1962/63 – FAIRS CUP

Rd 1	Copenhagen	(H)	W 4–0
Rd 1	Copenhagen	(A)	W 3–2
Rd 2	Utrecht	(A)	W 1–0
Rd 2	Utrecht	(H)	W 2–1
Rd 3	Valencia	(A)	L 0–5
Rd 3	Valencia	(H)	W 2–1

1965/66 – FAIRS CUP

Rd 1	Valencia	(H)	W 2–0
Rd 1	Valencia	(A)	L 0–2
Replay	Valencia	(A)	L 0–3

1967/68 – FAIRS CUP

Rd 1	Porto	(H)	W 3–0
Rd 1	Porto	(A)	L 1–3
Rd 2	Naples	(A)	L 1–4
Rd 2	Naples	(H)	W 5–0
Rd 3	Leeds United	(A)	L 0–1
Rd 3	Leeds United	(H)	D 1–1

1968/69 – FAIRS CUP

Rd 1	Olympia	(A)	W 3–0
Rd 1	Olympia	(H)	W 2–1
Rd 2	Lokomotiv Leipzig	(H)	W 3–1
Rd 2	Lokomotiv Leipzig	(A)	W 1–0
Rd 3	Hamburg	(A)	L 0–1
Rd 3	Hamburg	(H)	W 2–1

1970/71 – FAIRS CUP

Rd 1	Mälmo	(H)	W 6–0
Rd 1	Mälmo	(A)	W 3–2
Rd 2	Guimares	(H)	W 2–0
Rd 2	Guimares	(A)	L 1–2
Rd 3	Liverpool	(H)	L 0–1
Rd 3	Liverpool	(A)	L 0–2

1972/73 – CUP WINNERS CUP

Rd 1	Sporting Lisbon	(A)	L 1–2
Rd 1	Sporting Lisbon	(H)	W 6–1
Rd 2	FC Besa	(H)	W 7–1
Rd 2	FC Besa	(A)	D 1–1
Rd 3	Hadjuk Split	(H)	W 4–2
Rd 3	Hadjuk Split	(A)	L 0–3

1973/74 – UEFA CUP

Rd 1	Keflavik	(H)	W 2–0
Rd 1	Keflavik	(A)	D 1–1
Rd 2	Leeds United	(A)	D 0–0
Rd 2	Leeds United	(H)	D 0–0*

(*Hibs lost 5–4 on penalties)

1974/75 – UEFA CUP

Rd 1	Rosenborg	(A)	W 3–2
Rd 1	Rosenborg	(H)	W 9–1
Rd 2	Juventus	(H)	L 2–4
Rd 2	Juventus	(A)	L 0–4

1975/76 – UEFA CUP

| Rd 1 | Liverpool | (H) | W 1–0 |
| Rd 1 | Liverpool | (A) | L 1–3 |

1976/77 – UEFA CUP

Rd 1	Sochaux	(H)	W 1–0
Rd 1	Sochaux	(A)	D 0–0
Rd 2	Oesters	(H)	W 2–0
Rd 2	Oesters	(A)	L 1–4

1978/79 – UEFA CUP

Rd 1	Norrkoping	(H)	W 3–2
Rd 1	Norrkoping	(A)	D 0–0
Rd 2	Strasbourg	(A)	L 0–2
Rd 2	Strasbourg	(H)	W 1–0

1989/90 – UEFA Cup

Rd 1	Videoton	(H)	W 1–0
Rd 1	Videoton	(A)	W 3–0
Rd 2	Liege	(H)	D 0–0
Rd 2	Liege	(A)	L 0–1

1992/93 – UEFA CUP

| Rd 1 | Anderlecht | (H) | D 2–2 |
| Rd 1 | Anderlecht | (A) | D 1–1 |

2001/02 – UEFA CUP

| Rd 1 | AEK Athens | (A) | L 0–2 |
| Rd 1 | AEK Athens | (H) | W 3–2 |

APPENDIX X
FOUR OR MORE GOALS IN A GAME

Joe Baker (9)	Home v. Peebles Rovers, 11 February 1961 (Scottish Cup)
Gordon Smith (5)	Home v. Third Lanark, 8 November 1947 (League)
Joe Baker (5)	Home v. Third Lanark, 24 December 1960 (League)
Jock Weir (4)	Home v. Queen of the South, 10 August 1946 (League)
Jock Weir (4)	Away v. Alloa Athletic, 25 January 1947 (Scottish Cup)
Bobby Johnstone (4)	Home v. Airdrie, 27 August 1947 (League)
Gordon Smith (4)	Home v. Falkirk 10 December 1949 (League)
Eddie Turnbull (4)	Home v. Celtic 4 February 1950 (League)
Lawrie Reilly (4)	Home v. Falkirk, 9 September 1950 (League)
Lawrie Reilly (4)	Away v. Motherwell, 27 September 1952 (League)
Bobby Combe (4)	Away v. Airdrie, 28 February 1953 (League)
Joe Baker (4)	Away v. Hearts, 1 March 1958 (Scottish Cup)
Tommy Preston (4)	Away v. Airdrie, 24 October 1959 (League)
Joe Baker (4)	Home v. Airdrie, 20 August 1960 (League Cup)
Neil Martin (4)	Home v. Queen of the South, 7 March 1964 (League)
Neil Martin (4)	Home v. Falkirk, 2 January 1965 (League)
Neil Martin (4)	Home v. Falkirk, 25 September 1965 (League)
Neil Martin (4)	Home v. Alloa Athletic, 22 September 1965 (League Cup)
Jim Scott (4)	Home v. Alloa Athletic, 22 September 1965 (League Cup)
Arthur Duncan (4)	Home v. Falkirk, 23 October 1971 (League)
Alan Gordon (4)	Away v. Airdrie, 10 February 1973 (League)

Note that the above table does not include friendly fixtures.

Other titles published by Tempus

Hibernian Football Club 1875-1975
PAUL LUNNEY

This collection of around 200 archive photographs and items of memorabilia traces the history of one of Scotland's most famous clubs from its foundation in 1875 through the first 100 years of its history. Recalling championship successes, famous cup victories and star players, this brilliant pictorial account is a superb tribute to the players and triumphs of yesteryear.
0 7524 2170 0

Wizards and Bravehearts A History of the Scottish National Side
DAVID POTTER

The history of Scotland's national football team from 1872 is full of highs and lows, thrills and heartbreaks, passion and pride. Taking in thrilling World Cup campaigns and famous victories – notably over the Auld Enemy – the story has also featured many world-class players, such as Kenny Dalglish, Denis Law and Graeme Souness. This illustrated history records the ups and downs, the great characters and the classic games, and is essential reading for anyone with an interest in Scottish football.
0 7524 3183 8

Walter Sutherland Scottish Rugby Legend 1890-1918
KENNETH R. BOGLE

Walter Sutherland was one of the best and most popular Scottish rugby players of his generation. Blessed with natural speed and athleticism, was good enough to become a national sprint champion and to wear the Scottish athletics vest. Tragically, this magnificent footballer and athlete was destined to lose his life in the closing weeks of the First World War, aged only twenty-seven. This book, with a foreword by Bill McLaren, illustrates the nature of rugby football before the war and will fascinate anyone with an interest in the history of the game.
0 7524 3613 9

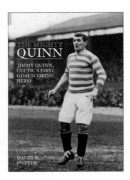

The Mighty Quinn Jimmy Quinn, Celtic's First Goalscoring Hero
DAVID W. POTTER

The powerful striker Jimmy Quinn became the hero of Scotland when in 1910 he almost single-handedly defeated England 2-0 to become the undisputed best player in Great Britain. Born in Croy in 1878 of illiterate Irish immigrants, he made over 300 appearances for Celtic, scoring 216 goals as Willie Maley's great Edwardian side won six League titles in a row. Some of the very essence of Scottish football lies here in the story of Jimmy Quinn.
0 7524 3460 8

If you are interested in purchasing other books published by Tempus, or in case you have difficulty finding any Tempus books in your local bookshop, you can also place orders directly through our website

www.tempus-publishing.com